Advance Praise for
From a Good Sales Call to a Great Sales Call

Once in a very long while, a book comes along that has the potential of changing the way people think about sales. Richard has written such a book. By examining why we lose the sale, he is able to show ways to win the deal. This is revolutionary, and a must read.

Stephan Schiffman
Bestselling author,
Cold Calling Techniques (That Really Work)

This is an incredibly insightful book that shows you special strategies to make more effective presentations and actually make more sales—faster and easier.

Brian Tracy
Bestselling author,
The Psychology of Selling

How can a salesperson win more business? Richard's book answers this question: by learning from lost sales. He delivers practical tools in a "how to" approach that will motivate and teach any salesperson to become a rainmaker. His concept is ground-breaking and empowering . . . a must-read for any sales executive or salesperson.

Jeffrey Fox
Bestselling author,
How to Become a Rainmaker

Very rarely is there anything "new" in the field of sales training, but Richard has captured something truly unique and innovative. This book is an absolute must for every sales manager and every salesperson who wants to stay on the cutting edge of influence. Richard clearly establishes himself as the "Thought Leader" in sales training with this book.

Peter Montoya
Author, *The Brand Called You*

From a Good
Sales Call
to a
GREAT
Sales Call

*Close More by Doing
What You Do Best*

RICHARD M. SCHRODER

New York Chicago San Francisco Lisbon London Madrid Mexico City
Milan New Delhi San Juan Seoul Singapore Sydney Toronto

ISBN: 978-0-07-171811-0
MHID: 0-07-171811-7

This publication is designed to provide accurate and authoritative information in regard to the subject matter covered. It is sold with the understanding that the publisher is not engaged in rendering legal, accounting, or other professional service. If legal advice or other expert assistance is required, the services of a competent professional person should be sought.

—From a declaration of principles jointly adopted by a committee of the American Bar Association and a committee of publishers

McGraw-Hill books are available at special quantity discounts to use as premiums and sales promotions or for use in corporate training programs. To contact a representative, please e-mail us at bulksales@mcgraw-hill.com.

Library of Congress Cataloging-in-Publication Data
Schroder, Richard M.
    From a good sales call to a great sales call : close more sales by doing what you do best / by Richard M. Schroder.
        p.   cm.
    ISBN 978-0-07-171811-0 (alk. paper)
    1. Selling.   2. Selling—Study and teaching.   3. Sales personnel—Training of.   I. Title.
    HF5438.25.8337   2011
    658.85—dc22
                                        2010024044

To Jeannine, Michael, and Molly

Contents

Foreword

Once in a very long while, a book comes along that has the potential of changing the way people think about sales. Richard has written such a book. By examining why we lose the sale, he is able to show ways to win the deal. This is revolutionary, and a must-read. Here's why.

For the longest time, I have wondered why salespeople never seem to understand what's really happened in their meetings with prospects. I once said that when a salesperson left the prospect's office, she seemed to disappear down a hole. Kind of like Alice in Wonderland, she kept dropping further down, only to emerge at the bottom of the hole to sign the deal. I believe that is what most folks think happens to salespeople.

That's not to say that salespeople didn't understand if they "got the sale" or "lost the sale." They just seem to be in the dark as to what really took place. They had no clue *why* calls resulted in drastically different outcomes.

In their minds, they went into this mysterious place called The Office. Once there, they undertook some sort of magical incantation. If all went well and the planets were aligned, they emerged with a signed contract. Sometimes, of course, they left the session empty-handed. But if I, or anyone else, asked what happened, their answers were filled with shrugs and confused expressions.

Most odd, they seemed to bear an animosity toward the individual to whom they were selling. They acted as if the prospect were the biggest obstacle to the sale. As if that person wasn't real but just an abstraction called The Client. And evidently to both parties the sales experience seemed surreal.

Having been a buyer and a seller, the veteran of thousands of such meetings, I thought I knew what took place in The Office. But somehow I could never put my finger on the heart of the process. But as I thought about it, more and more, an answer emerged from the fog.

On those occasions when the sale didn't happen, especially if I was the client conveying the news, salespeople would ask me why. For a long time, I gave the tired (and lame) answer that the price wasn't right, the color was wrong, or we did not need the product at the time.

The fact of the matter is that I wasn't being entirely candid with the salesperson, and not because I had anything to hide. The price not being right or the color being wrong could very well have been part of the equation, but there was missing information from my response. What I neglected to comment on was the impact (or lack of impact) that the salesperson's performance had on the deal.

Additionally, in many instances, *the salesperson is competing against the status quo.* The prospect has something that fits the bill already and is using it satisfactorily.

Either way, when prospects give salespeople feedback on lost sales, buyers often focus on the mechanics of the product (i.e., product features or pricing issues) instead of what's truly important: the relationship between the seller and the buyer. This is a very real problem for most salespeople, and this book will help you to overcome this issue so that you can truly understand what goes on during your time in The Office.

Another problem I've grappled with over the years is defining what exactly the salesperson *does.* You'd think it would be pretty straightforward, wouldn't you? With 21 million salespeople in this country, you'd imagine they have some idea of what fills their days. But part of the challenge of sales today is that salespeople are trying to redefine their positions. They struggle with all sorts of terms and definitions.

One expression I hate is "drum beater." It conjures up an image that people associate with salespeople. Someone who's a backslapper and a hand grabber. An apple polisher, with a mouth full of gleaming teeth. Not a group to inspire confidence, are we?

Movies like *Tin Man* and *Glengarry, Glen Ross*, not to mention the television show *Mad Men*, help perpetuate the image of the slick salesperson without ethics, someone who never revisits the prospect's home, much less office, again.

On the contrary, I believe that *great* salespeople have a strong ethical code. That's precisely what makes them great. But this is something that needs, desperately, to be taught to the new generation of salespeople.

Can sales be learned, or are there people who are just born to sell? You know the kind: people with the gift of gab, who can sell you the Brooklyn Bridge. (Yes, it was resold recently!) In fact, I believe that great salespeople are bred, not born. And good salespeople are easy to find.

Yes, that's right! *A good salesperson is easy to find.* Follow my logic now: There are so many bad salespeople that the good ones stick out. They win the awards from the company, they are at the job for a long time, and they seem to relish in the position of selling king.

The bad ones knock on doors over and over again. They may have 10 different jobs before they leave the sales profession and move into management, where they screw up the works.

There seem to be four areas that concern even the most average of salespeople:

* They need to knock on doors or prospect.
* They need to be able to make a presentation.
* They need to understand their product.
* They need to have a sales personality.

With prospecting, the salesperson will try everything to get the appointment. He will cold call on the telephone, try mailing cute postcards, and meet you at a trade show. And once he has his jaw into you, he will never let go.

I once knew a woman who threatened to faint unless her contact came down from his office and escorted her upstairs. He refused; she fainted and was escorted out of the building by security. (But at least she tried.) There must be some truth to the story about the guy who mailed his contact a shoe, stating, "Now I've got a foot in the door, let me in!" Over and over, the challenge is the same: get the sale, by any means necessary!

How much ability does the salesperson have to have to make a successful presentation? The answer turns out to be simple: *just enough to make the sale.* And here's the key to this: *how much does the client need the product?* If the person truly needs the product, the worst presentation on the face of earth will sell the damn thing.

I was at a presentation at a major broadcasting company when the computer went out. For three hours the presenters worked on getting this gadget to work, but the electrical power would not work for them. Promptly at 10 a.m., the secretary came into the room and turned off the timer. The electricity came back on, and with it the computer.

The point here is not to rely on technology, not to rely on gimmicks, not to rely on smoke and mirrors. What counts in the end is whether the product or service solves a crucial problem for the client.

As an effective salesperson, you need to know that. You don't need to know *how* it solves the problem. This may seem paradoxical, but it's crucial to the success of your sale. After all, how many people know how a computer works? Or how a smartphone works? The point is, what problem does it solve? If you know that, you can sell it. It's that simple.

Finally, we come to the winning sales personality. Almost every sales test ever given assesses this. Without the winning sales personality, there is no salesperson. There will be no prospecting, and there will be no presentation and no sale. Clear and simple. No sales personality, no sales. It's that simple.

The key lies in a basic slogan: "Nothing happens until somebody sells something." Of course, it cannot be that simple. A sale is an *interaction* between people (one in which both win). A sale is an act of communication, something that has a give and take. However, too often it misses a crucial element: the need to be frank and honest.

It's my considered opinion (considered after more than 35 years of sales experience) that the problems of sales today, nine times out of ten, lie in the training of salespeople. Instead of concentrating on the mechanics of selling, we have to focus on the relationship between seller and client. We have to constantly ask ourselves, when we walk out of a room, "What happened in there? Did I convince the client? Did I build a lasting link? Did I make a connection that's going to endure?"

From the constant examination and reexamination of these questions, we'll find the answer to what makes a great sale. And readers of *From a Good Sales Call to a Great Sales Call* will go a long way down the road to answering those questions.

Stephan Schiffman

Acknowledgments

When I first sat down to write the acknowledgments and reflect on everyone who helped me write this book, I was amazed at how many people had been instrumental in the development of this project. No one publishes a book without the help of other people.

As I worked with each person, I learned a tremendous amount about the sales process, my work, and my company. In his or her own way, each person helped to stretch and organize my thinking and writing, which allowed me to take my research and expertise to a whole new level. Bruce Springsteen once suggested that we write about what we are trying to figure out, and writing a book truly does give you clarity on your subject matter.

I would like to thank the following people for all their help:

My wife, Jeannine, for your support, encouragement, and for being so understanding about all the time it took to write the book. I never would have finished without all those Sundays to write. Thank you for all the hours of discussion and for helping me to develop my writing career. Love to Michael and Molly.

Heather Jenkins, my business partner, for your collaboration and tireless editing on the many drafts of this book. The research you performed on all of our sales data was integral in developing the book. Thank you for being such a great sounding board and for being the trusted first set of eyes on all the writing.

Ted Weinstein, my literary agent, for believing in this project from the beginning and for being my publishing industry guide. It was your insight that allowed me to look at my work from a different perspective and take the book concept to a whole new level. You are a true professional, and this book never would have happened without you. Thank you for responding to my initial query letter and for finding the right publisher for the project.

Stephan Schiffman, my favorite sales author, for writing the foreword, but more importantly for being such a great mentor to me during this process. There were many times you helped me and asked nothing in return, and I greatly appreciate it. I have been a fan of your work for so many years, and I have learned a lot from your books. You are a prolific writer, and I am just glad I was able to find a sales topic you have not covered!

Donya Dickerson, senior editor at McGraw-Hill, for believing in the project and for publishing the book. I appreciate your being the champion for this book within McGraw-Hill. Your editorial feedback was tremendously helpful; it gave the book great clarity and made it much easier to read.

Rose Vignola, my sister-in-law and part-time research pro, for all your help with marketing my writing to agents, magazines, and publishers. Your steadfast work on this project helped me not only find the right agent, but your efforts also educated me on the publishing industry (which ultimately led to this book being published). I never would have found Ted Weinstein without you.

Jim Bowley, for your friendship and valuable critique of the book. Your knowledge and experience in sales, writing, and win/loss analysis offered powerful insights to the book's concept. Thank you for all the time and effort you put into reading and offering suggestions on my work. I have truly appreciated your writing counsel over the years.

Geza Szurovy, for your wisdom, insight, and mentorship. You taught me a lot about the writing process, and, most importantly, you taught me that it can be done.

Andrew Cloutier, for all your help with editing the book. I appreciate your rigorous efforts. Your wordsmithing and critique helped take the book to a whole new level.

Tom Johnson, for our many discussions about the sales process over the years. Thank you for your advice and friendship.

Everyone at Anova Consulting Group, for all your hard work in making our win/loss analysis program such a success. Without all of your research and insight, this book would not have been possible. Special thanks to Lisa Reibstein and George Radford.

All my clients. As always, thank you for your business and for allowing my company to serve your sales teams and help them improve their sales effectiveness.

Finally, my mom, dad, brother, and sister for all your support.

Introduction

This book is the result of more than 12 years of research on the sales process. Over this time, I have personally managed hundreds of win/loss analysis studies for Fortune 500 sales teams throughout the country, and I have been involved in conducting thousands of interviews with prospects on behalf of salespeople for both won and lost sales situations. I have also surveyed, interviewed, and consulted with hundreds of salespeople and sales managers about why they win and lose in new business situations.

As I worked with sales teams and read through interview transcript after interview transcript, I began to realize that salespeople often unknowingly make the same mistakes and frequently lose for the same reasons year in and year out. As I continued to perform this research, I became increasingly passionate about the pursuit of educating salespeople on how to better understand why they win and lose so that they can ultimately increase their win rate.

One thing that has always stood out to me is that there typically are only two or three reasons one sales rep wins a deal over another (the historical average from my research is actually 2.5 reasons that a prospect cites as to why a particular salesperson loses a deal). In horse racing, the winning horse typically wins by less than a second, and the sales profession is similar. In an increasingly competitive business climate, salespeople must continuously sharpen their selling skills in order to get ahead of the competition and win more business.

I have come to realize that the very best way to show salespeople how to improve their sales effectiveness is by helping them learn why they win and lose, so that they can reinforce their successful behaviors and rectify the selling deficiencies that are holding them back. It is only after salespeople obtain accurate and candid feedback on their sales performance that they can institute meaningful change.

This book will show you how to enhance your selling skills by learning about a critical piece of the sales process that has been largely overlooked by most salespeople, sales managers, and sales trainers. It will show you how to effectively debrief with prospects after buying decisions have been made. This book will also show you why it can be so difficult to gather candid prospect feedback, what can be gained by improving your postdecision debrief process, and how to properly implement your own win/loss analysis program at the end of your sales process.

This book is quite different from other sales books, because most sales books focus only on the technical aspects of selling through the close. Although these books are quite useful, they do not cover a very important final component of the sales process. Most sales books and sales training manuals break out the sales process into key components such as prospecting, establishing a connection, identifying needs, presenting, answering questions and handling objections, and closing the sale. Yet the vast majority of these books do not cover the final element of the sales process: debriefing with prospects postdecision.

Although this process has not traditionally been an area of focus, sales professionals have always debriefed with prospects. Many salespeople attempt to figure out why they win and lose business, and many ask prospects for this information. However, even though this element of the sales process has been practiced, the reality is that most salespeople are only scratching the surface when they question prospects at the end of a sales cycle. Postsale debriefing is largely performed incorrectly or inadequately, and a failure to grasp the true drivers of the purchase decision has prevented many salespeople from truly improving their selling skills. This book will show you how to perform a much more comprehensive debrief to garner detailed, candid, and actionable information.

If you are like most salespeople, you are occasionally performing some type of debrief at the end of your sales cycles. Therefore, it is not a matter of having the time to do this type of exercise; it is more about how you can learn to perform this process more productively and comprehensively to get actual results. That's what this book is all about.

This book is for salespeople, entrepreneurs, or anyone who sells as part of their job who wants to make a long-term commitment to their personal careers. This book is also for anyone who is involved in managing a sales team, product and marketing managers, or those responsible for running a business.

This book presents a simple and practical eight-step program to help you learn how to debrief better with prospects postdecision and ultimately increase your close rate:

Step 1: Discover the Benefits of Successfully Debriefing with Prospects

Step 2: Understand the Postdecision Mind-Set of the Prospect

Step 3: Recognize How Salespeople Can Inhibit the Feedback Process

Step 4: Design a Prospect Debrief Questionnaire

Step 5: Utilize Proven Interviewing Techniques for Conducting Debrief Calls

Step 6: Identify and Analyze Your Win/Loss Trends

Step 7: Benchmark Your Feedback

Step 8: Implement the Right Techniques to Increase Your Close Rate

This program offers a proven process that will enable you to make a firmer commitment to continuous improvement over time. This program will allow you to learn not only the reasons you lose business but also the reasons you win. Once you learn how to gather this information on an ongoing basis, you will be better able to mitigate your own unique sales process deficiencies and maximize your strengths. By implementing this eight-step program, you will be well on your way to closing more business and earning more money.

Remember, if you are not getting better at selling, you are most likely getting worse. In anything you do, the only way to improve your performance is to identify the true reasons for failure and implement solutions to fix them. This program is for people who want to take their sales careers to the next level and who aren't afraid to seek out and learn from candid feedback. This program is *not* for those who want to maintain the status quo in their sales process. It is not for salespeople who are not totally committed to their profession and who aren't passionate about what they do. If you don't want to work on yourself and think you already know everything there is to learn about selling, put this book back on the shelf. This book is about learning how to get better at selling by not hiding from the truth.

PART 1

. . . .

RECOGNIZING THE HIDDEN OPPORTUNITY TO INCREASE YOUR CLOSE RATE

. . . .

Discover the Benefits of Successfully Debriefing with Prospects

Understanding why a deal is won or lost is critical, yet most salespeople have little (if any) understanding of the true reasons for winning and losing. The first question salespeople ask themselves when they lose a sale is, "Why did I lose?" Though the question may be straightforward, getting an accurate answer can be quite difficult.

Salespeople often ask prospects why they lost a deal, but they don't typically get a straight answer. According to proprietary sales research data, prospects share the complete truth less than half of the time! This means that in a majority of new business situations, salespeople do not have a complete and accurate understanding of why they lost, causing them to miss a critical opportunity to improve their sales performance, better understand their competitive landscape, enhance their company's products and services, and ultimately increase sales.

Every year, companies spend significant time and money training their salespeople. However, most companies do little to verify that salespeople are actually implementing the right tactics in their interactions with prospects. Most companies do not tie their sales training to actual data and feedback from prospects, and this is a huge lost opportunity for salespeople to improve their selling efforts. This disconnect between salespeople and actual customer feedback is a key factor for why most sales forecasts are wrong, and it shows that there is a significant opportunity for salespeople to improve their

Figure 1.1   Salesperson's Stated Perceptions for Losing versus Actual Prospect Reasons

new business win rates. In an increasingly competitive world, every deal counts.

Over the past decade, I have been involved in more than 200 win/loss analysis studies. My firm has conducted thousands of interviews in a variety of industries with bids lost and bids won prospects on behalf of our Fortune 500 clients. As part of these studies, we have matched up the reasons that sales reps provided for why they lost specific deals versus the actual reasons provided by prospects to us as an independent third party. As Figure 1.1 illustrates, only 40 percent of the time did sales reps have an accurate, full realization of why they lost. Another 28 percent of the time, the salespeople had some of the story correct but were missing other key factors that contributed to the loss, and the remaining 32 percent of the time, the sales reps were totally wrong in their assessments of why they lost the deal.

Additionally, as Figure 1.2 illustrates, salespeople's own perceptions generally align with these percentages. The average salesperson believes that he or she got the truth from a prospect 43 percent of the time. This demonstrates that salespeople are reasonably adept at judging when prospects are being honest with them. However, sales reps underestimate the amount of time that prospects provide

Sales reps' understanding of why deal was won or lost is. . .	Actual % based on research	Sales reps' perceptions	% Differential
Complete and accurate	40%	43%	Slight overestimate
Partially correct but some of the story is unknown	28%	37%	Overestimate by 9 percentage points
Completely wrong	32%	20%	Underestimate by 12 percentage points

Figure 1.2 Comparison of Sales Reps' Perceptions of Prospect Candor versus Actual Candor

completely false information. Sales reps estimate that prospects withhold the truth 20 percent of the time; in reality, this occurs 32 percent of the time.

This situation does not exist only for lost deals but also for bids-won situations. Most salespeople don't have a good handle on why they win business, either, because many salespeople do not even bother to ask prospects why. In fact, only 40 percent of the time does the average salesperson ask a new customer why he or she won the deal. This means that the majority of salespeople have a limited understanding of the true reasons why they win in the first place. True, they may have their own opinions as to why they are successful at winning business, but they have not verified these reasons with prospects. Instead, most salespeople celebrate when they win a new piece of business and simply move on to the next deal. What they don't understand is that they are missing out on a key opportunity to better understand their strengths and areas for improvement in the eyes of prospects who have bought from them.

This data begs the question, if salespeople don't truly understand why they win and lose, how are they expected to improve their performance? As I tracked these types of sales process statistics over time, it became startling to realize the frequency with which salespeople miss out on key feedback that is instrumental to their success. This dilemma is the impetus for this book and explains why 90 percent of salespeople believe they could improve upon how they debrief with prospects postdecision in order to receive more candid feedback.

This book will teach you how to gather more accurate and meaningful postdecision feedback from your prospects, and this feedback will allow you to focus on your strengths and self-diagnose and address your individual areas for improvement during the sales process.

> 90 percent of salespeople believe they could improve upon how they debrief with prospects postdecision in order to receive more candid feedback.

However, before you learn the many techniques to better debrief with prospects postdecision, it is important to first understand why this is such a complex problem for so many salespeople. In Part 1 of this book, we will explore both the benefits that can be obtained by implementing your own win/loss analysis system as well as the challenges that salespeople face as they debrief with prospects postdecision.

Let's begin by exploring the transformational benefits that can be achieved by successfully implementing a comprehensive postdecision debrief process at the end of your sales cycle.

APPLY FEEDBACK TO YOUR ENTIRE SALES PROCESS

There are many reasons conducting in-depth debriefs with prospects will be valuable to you, but the best reason is that by committing to this process, you will ultimately improve your sales effectiveness and increase your close rate. This will occur because conducting win/loss reviews will allow you to develop your own self-improvement training program by applying prospect feedback across all areas of your sales process.

To illustrate this point, let's explore how debriefing with a prospect fits into the entire sales process. As shown in Figure 1.3, conventional sales wisdom suggests that there are several key areas to the sales process, including getting in the door, establishing a connection, conducting a needs analysis, presenting, answering questions and handling objections, and closing. However, correctly debriefing with a prospect at the conclusion of the sales process is the often overlooked final element and is not only educational but critical if you want to win more business and maximize your earning potential.

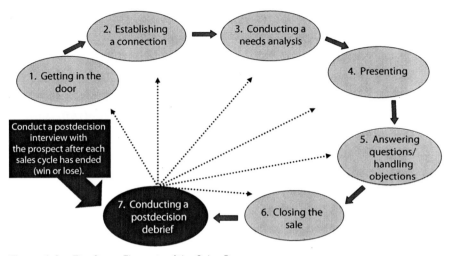

Figure 1.3   The Seven Elements of the Sales Process

Over time, the process of gathering feedback on won and lost situations will change your sales behavior as you apply what has been learned from these discussions to the other areas of your sales process in future sales opportunities. Win/loss analysis allows for a very valuable element where typical sales training falls short: the constant use of feedback as a driver of behavioral change. By getting direct, personalized feedback from prospects, you will be able to self-diagnose and mitigate your own sales process deficiencies and improve upon your strengths, often in real time.

> Conducting win/loss reviews will allow you to develop your own self-improvement training program by applying prospect feedback across all areas of your sales process.

IMPLEMENT EFFECTIVE AND ACTIONABLE TACTICS

Although 60 percent of salespeople indicate they receive some form of sales training each year, many never apply what they learn from their sales training in their daily interactions with prospects (and it is only through application and practice that sales tactics get learned). In fact, studies have shown that most salespeople forget the majority of what they learn at training sessions within 48 hours. Therefore, by learning to obtain better and more candid feedback from prospects, salespeople can apply their learning back into their sales process. It is much easier for salespeople to incorporate feedback from the concrete, real-life experience of a lost or won prospect than it is for them to remember abstract sales tactics from training seminars.

When you begin to hear direct, personalized feedback from prospects on a continuous basis and you start to notice trends in what your prospects are telling you, you will be more likely to learn from your mistakes and change your behavior. It may sting at first, but it will sink in faster than if you were simply listening to a training session about general sales tactics. In fact, the combination of win/loss analysis followed up by targeted sales training can be incredibly effective at improving your close rate, but you must first understand your main sales process issues before you embark on tailored sales training. This is what most sales professionals don't do. They don't first assess their own unique challenges before trying to implement a solution.

This is analogous to trying to sell a prospect on your product or service before you fully understand the prospect's unique needs. As you know, it is much easier to make the sale if you understand what the prospect's true needs are. Similarly, you shouldn't try to fix your own sales problems with training until you have accurately identified your unique selling challenges.

The training/feedback disconnect is not necessarily the fault of each individual salesperson, as it is often the responsibility of the companies that provide training to their sales force at annual conferences. Since most companies do not perform win/loss analysis first, sales management typically does not have an accurate understanding of the true reasons their sales teams win and lose. Therefore, when sales training is provided, it often does not generate the highest impact or ROI because it is not targeted toward the specific and unique needs of the sales team and each individual member.

This is not to say that sales training is not critical. Sales training can be a very valuable motivational and educational tool that can be used to augment your arsenal of sales tactics. However, sales training is more valuable if you apply what you've learned and you apply the right tactics to your own unique selling deficiencies. Conducting enhanced postdecision debriefs will allow you as a salesperson to better understand what lessons you need to learn and how to better apply them.

Just as a doctor should not prescribe a medication or treatment to a patient until she has made an accurate diagnosis of the problem, salespeople should make sure they understand the main areas where they need help before making changes to their sales process. This is what win/loss analysis does; it creates an ongoing improvement flywheel and allows you to continuously get better at your profession. Sales training is critical, but it is best when performed after an accurate diagnosis is made.

TAKE RESPONSIBILITY FOR WHY YOU WIN AND LOSE

One thing I have always noticed when working with salespeople and sales leaders is that when I ask if they know the true reasons why they win and lose, they often respond in the same way. They pause for a moment, and then most say they are really not sure. They eventually come up with a few reasons, but most aren't fully sure of all the reasons, and very few can come up with the correct proportions of the reasons behind winning and losing. In fact, very few salespeople can rank order the reasons they win or lose. Can you see the problem with this scenario? If you don't fully understand the problem, how can you implement a solution?

There is an old saying that goes like this: *Looking for the solution without listening to the problem is working in the dark.* This is what most salespeople are doing. They continue to sell day by day without fully understanding why they win and lose business, and therefore they cannot work on their own sales deficiencies.

Most salespeople, when asked why they win and lose, will mention product or service features, or pricing issues. Very few will accept responsibility and admit that their sales performance could be improved. In most win/loss studies, the sales process is typically a top driver of the purchase decision. As I'll show in Chapter 2, most salespeople are wrong in their assessments of how much they impact the outcome of a deal.

One way to think about this situation is by looking at the sales process as "binary." In each sales situation, you either win or lose—it's that simple. Therefore, each sales situation is really a pass/fail exercise, and it is up to each salesperson to better understand how to pass more tests. By conducting more candid debriefs with prospects, you will learn the reasons you are passing and failing and, ultimately, how to address the obstacles.

In some cases, you can also lose to "no decision," when the prospect chooses to defer the decision or maintain the status quo (i.e., choosing to do nothing or electing to remain with a current supplier). However, losing a deal to no decision (or the status quo) is still a loss. It is a loss because you were unable to convince the prospect to make a move, and thus you did not do a good enough job to motivate him to make a change. Therefore, the binary analogy still holds. A no decision is really a loss, or a failing grade.

As you can probably tell, I am asking you to change how you approach selling because I am expecting you to take full responsibility for everything about your sales process. You must accept full accountability in order to be successful. I have found that the very best salespeople in any industry are the ones who take full responsibility for every step of the sales cycle.

The best salespeople don't see losing as an inevitable process that can't be changed. Winning salespeople work to learn everything they can about why they win and lose, and they are constantly improving themselves. They believe they are in control and can learn from their mistakes to succeed in the future.

The bottom performers are typically the ones who will say it's all about chemistry and there is nothing they can do to work on themselves to change the outcome. These people don't believe the outcomes they achieve in life have anything to do with their own behavior. They essentially feel powerless to alter whatever life brings their way.

As a salesperson, you must become an optimist and take full responsibility for the sales process and making sure the prospect is totally satisfied with the whole experience. One way to ensure this is to look at debriefing with a prospect as if you were conducting a prospect satisfaction study. Just as companies often conduct client or customer satisfaction surveys, why shouldn't you as a salesperson conduct your own prospect satisfaction survey? This way you can fully understand the top drivers of prospect satisfaction and the most critical pain points. Just as client satisfaction analysis is intended to ultimately increase retention, prospect satisfaction analysis will help you increase your close rate.

Salespeople and companies should be just as worried about prospect satisfaction as they are about customer satisfaction. In fact, companies should be more concerned with prospect satisfaction, because bringing in customers is one of the most important and costly tasks in business. Companies spend a lot of time and money surveying to see if customers are happy, but most don't check to see how satisfied prospects are with the sales process. The process of surveying only customers creates a customer-focused distortion that can make organizations conservative and limit their ability to really understand the competitive market dynamics with which they are dealing. True market dynamics can be more accurately gleaned from *prospective* customers, because prospects who have recently reviewed their options are typically more knowledgeable of the latest competitive and market

> **Salespeople and companies should be just as worried about prospect satisfaction as they are about customer satisfaction.**

trends than existing customers. Gauging prospect satisfaction is a huge, untapped opportunity for most companies to increase their growth rate.

If you want to be the best salesperson you can be, you must train yourself to be committed to prospect satisfaction. After all, prospects are your customers. They are the ones who pay your bills through the commissions you earn when you obtain them as customers for your company. Therefore, in order to grow as a salesperson, you must work more effectively with prospects.

We are all familiar with ever-rising quotas and higher hurdle rates for sales success. In the corporate world, there continues to be a push toward promoting as much sales activity as possible. As a result of these factors, many salespeople are trained to shrug off a win or loss and quickly move on to the next deal. A common sales management paradigm is one in which salespeople are expected to

> Gauging prospect satisfaction is a huge, untapped opportunity for most companies to increase their growth rate.

hold as many sales meetings as possible. There is some validity to this approach, because it is true that the more qualified prospects you are out in front of, the more you will sell. In general, if you double the number of qualified prospects you get in front of, you will most likely double your sales. However, like anything else in life, there is a middle ground between quality and quantity. What many inexperienced salespeople do is take as many meetings as possible, when another option to increase sales performance is to improve the quality of each sales meeting. One proven way to improve the quality of meetings is to continuously incorporate prospect feedback into your sales process. Some salespeople view postdecision debriefs as a less fruitful use of their time than moving on to the next deal. However, as this book will show, win rates can be increased by using feedback from in-depth postdecision interviews. Wouldn't you rather meet with fewer people and win more business?

When you learn how to properly debrief with a prospect, you will shine a light on the situation. You will find that once you get a better understanding of why you win and lose, you will be in a much better position to execute changes to your sales process.

IMPROVE THE EFFECTIVENESS OF YOUR SALES PRESENTATIONS AND SALES TEAM

As you begin to gather comprehensive feedback from prospects, the information will influence how you prepare and execute on your sales presentations, and it will change how you conduct yourself during sales meetings.

As an example, lack of customization of a sales presentation is a key reason salespeople lose in new business situations. One way you can combat this is to learn from lost prospects what kind of customization would be most effective. For instance, prospects will often share with you how the competition customized their pitch and won the business. This will allow you to learn from others and increase your abilities in future deal situations.

Another reason prospects often mention is that one sales rep was not as prepared as another. When you begin to gather candid feedback, you may find that you are not coming across as prepared compared to others. This feedback will highlight specific behaviors that caused the winning sales rep to come across as well-prepared and can help you improve your preparation skills before sales meetings.

Feedback is also critical for other presentation team members. In team selling situations, win/loss reviews can pinpoint how your sales team can present in a more cohesive manner. When presenting as a group, it is often hard to understand where your team is strong and weak. However, prospects are in a great position to comment on areas for improvement, as well as what they see as your team's strong points.

If you are responsible for quarterbacking any type of team selling situation, win/loss reviews will help you understand what you need to do to prepare your sales team before each presentation. This process is not a witch hunt. It is not about pointing out each sales team member's flaws. Instead, it is about allowing you as the sales team leader to gather insights and red flags that you can use to better assign and prepare your teams.

Whenever a group presents together, there will always be some members who are better than others in any given type of presentation format. This distinction is especially clear in situations where client service team members or operational or technology personnel are brought in to present alongside more seasoned sales personnel. This is a tough challenge for any sales organization, because unlike salespeople, service and operations personnel tend to be more internally focused and are not used to spending time in front of audiences. In fact, they may have taken their job because they do not like being in a sales role and prefer to be in a more supportive function within the organization. However, the problem for sales professionals in team-selling situations is that the team is only as strong as its weakest link.

In the research my company has done, we have found that during team-selling situations, prospects and committee members often pay more attention to how well the client service people present themselves. Understandably, prospects are trying to get a gauge on who they will ultimately be working with and how comfortable they will be in this working relationship, so they tend to pay less attention to the salespeople and more attention to the service personnel. They tend to place more weight on what service and day-to-day contacts think than on what salespeople think.

Therefore, if you are involved in this type of complex sales situation, it is your responsibility to coach the other members of your sales team. Win/loss reviews are a critical tool to add to your arsenal, because when you get prospect feedback on the cohesiveness of your team's presentation, you will be in a much better position to make tweaks to better prepare in the future. It is really your job to get your team functioning at as high a level as possible. Remember, that is why you get paid the big bucks. It is your responsibility to bring out the best in your team and to make everyone else look as strong as possible. This is a tough skill to learn, and win/loss reviews are a very helpful tool in helping you understand how well you are doing at this function.

DETERMINE KEY DRIVERS FOR CLOSING NEW BUSINESS

Another valuable benefit of properly conducting a postdecision debrief is that it will give you a better insight into prospects' decision making drivers. This is perhaps one of the most valuable areas on which to gather feedback, because correctly identifying your prospect's unique needs is the most critical element of the sales process. What other area of the sales process is more important than this? If you were able to determine each of your prospects' needs 100 percent of the time, you would be able to close many more deals.

> One of the main reasons sales are lost is that the salesperson does not accurately uncover and understand the prospect's unique needs.

One of the main reasons sales are lost is that the salesperson does not accurately uncover and understand the prospect's unique needs. By asking the prospect this question during the debrief, you will be able to match up the real prospect drivers with what you thought they were. Over time, this process will allow you to better gauge what prospects are looking for during the sales process, and this will allow you to provide a more customized presentation.

By committing to a process of conducting postmortems on each sales situation and learning each prospect's key needs, you will eventually gain a better sense of what prospects are looking for in new sales situations. As you debrief with individual prospects (both wins and losses), you will learn why they made their decisions, and this will allow you to better position your team, your products and services, and yourself in the future.

UNCOVER UNMET PROSPECT/CUSTOMER NEEDS

Debriefing with prospects is not only about learning how you can improve your sales performance; it is also about learning how your company's products and services can be improved and what key features your company is not providing that customers would like to see. Just as important, understanding the market's objective view of your products may help you prioritize selling efforts on specific capabilities or sales verticals where differentiation is highest and where you may have the highest probability for wins.

This area represents one feedback element that can be very easily obtained from prospects. There is less of a personal involvement for prospects when they are giving you feedback on your company's products and services. Prospects are generally more candid giving feedback about product and service deficiencies than they are giving feedback on salespeople.

This is why many salespeople overemphasize a product or service deficiency as a reason for loss. Prospects often feel more comfortable giving negative feedback on a product, service, price, or brand image because it is less personal. This is why when salespeople ask for feedback, they tend to get skewed results that do not factor in salesmanship. Another reason for this phenomenon is that many prospects are not salespeople, but they are typically product

> Prospects are generally more candid giving feedback about product and service deficiencies than they are giving feedback on salespeople.

experts. They are people who use your product or service every day, so they know a lot about how to distinguish between your product and that of your competition.

Product feedback can also be very valuable to entrepreneurs who want to grow their businesses by learning from won and lost sales situations. As an entrepreneur, you always will have direct responsibility and control over your product or services.

By performing this type of detailed due diligence exercise on your won and lost prospects, you may also find that your company is behind the marketplace in terms of your products and services. You may realize that it will be impossible for your company to catch up to some of the leading providers from a product development standpoint. This can be a tricky situation for salespeople, who typically have limited control over product changes, because it may force them to think more strongly about moving to another firm where many of the product/service objections may be overcome more easily due to a stronger offering. Either way, this is still a benefit to you, because it is always better to have the most accurate and comprehensive understanding of where your company stands in the marketplace. Whether you change firms or stick it out, you will have a much better chance at winning if you totally understand all of your company's product or service challenges.

ENHANCE PRODUCT DEVELOPMENT

By gathering comprehensive feedback on product and service deficiencies, you will be in a much better position to relay this information internally to your company. As a salesperson, you are exposed to the most cutting edge information pertaining to your marketplace. Every day, you are out speaking with customers and prospects who drive where your industry is going and influence the most critical product development areas. By more accurately understanding prospect, product, or service needs, you can make your company stronger by relaying more accurate feedback to the senior management, product development, technology, and marketing areas of your company.

Since salespeople are out with customers and prospects all the time, they do tend to develop a keen sense of what is going on in the marketplace, and they are often the first to hear about new enhancements being made by the competition. Depending on a company's organizational structure, it may be the sales team's job to educate the rest of the company on what is going on in the marketplace because sales is often in the best position to do so. However, salespeople may not have the full, unbiased story, so they often unknowingly disseminate incomplete or inaccurate information within their organizations. Since 60 percent of the time salespeople do not get an accurate picture of why they lose, it would stand to reason that prospect information being circulated around most companies is inexact the majority of the time.

> **Since 60 percent of the time salespeople do not get an accurate picture of why they lose, it would stand to reason that prospect information being circulated around most companies is inexact the majority of the time.**

As faulty feedback and information spreads throughout companies, it can ultimately corrupt decision making. Over time, senior managers start making decisions based on inaccurate information derived from prospects who were not fully candid and salespeople who are not in an objective position to share unbiased information. By learning how to properly debrief with prospects, you will ultimately be able to share more accurate and valuable information within your company.

GATHER COMPETITIVE INTELLIGENCE

When you are in a sales situation with a prospect and you are selling against the competition, you will typically learn a lot about what other players are doing and where and how your product stacks up against competitors. However, it is really during the postdecision debrief where you can catapult your learning about the competition. Prospects are less likely to reveal competitive intelligence during the sales process because they feel more of a sense of obligation to the other competing firms, almost like they are referees and they need to be fair and impartial to all sides. However, once the sales process is over, prospects are more likely to share where you and your company's products and services fell short.

During the sales process, most prospects are not going to tell you where you are not competitive with respect to the competition. It's your job to figure it out. That is, unless you know the prospect well and she is going to choose you either way. In these cases, the prospect will share everything with you in order to help you win the deal. The postdecision debrief is the best place to gather competitive intelligence because prospects will be more at ease, and also, if you position the discussion properly, you can use the guilt of the loss to extract valuable information that you can use in future situations. As you learn to gather competitive intelligence at the end of each sales process, you will develop a more thorough understanding of each competitor, ultimately allowing you to better differentiate your company in future sales situations.

CHAPTER WRAP-UP

All of these benefits will provide you with a lasting and powerful component to add to your sales process, which will allow you to develop a strategic advantage over the competition. In business, everything around you is, in a sense, constantly changing. The competition is continually evolving as new products are developed daily and new strategies are being implemented in your marketplace. Your current customers and references are being heavily courted by your competitors. Your best customer references may be leaving to take on new jobs, or there might be newer and younger salespeople who are coming in who are willing to work harder than you. If you don't keep up, you can very quickly find yourself falling behind. Over time, your business and abilities will erode if you don't continually reinvent yourself and grow your skill sets.

The good news is that you as a salesperson can work on yourself easily because you don't need to attain feedback from your superiors or from anywhere else within your company (like others who are not interfacing with customers). You can instead get feedback directly from your most important source: prospects. As a salesperson, you do not need to be held back by whether your company has a formal mechanism for training and feedback. You can do it yourself. But you have to want to get it, and you have to want to calibrate your understanding of your abilities with what they actually are. You can always do better, and you should never stop in your pursuit of excellence. Leave stagnation to others. After all, you wouldn't be reading this book if you didn't want to improve your abilities.

In sales, you must take responsibility for your own success. You entered into this contract when you started your sales career and when you accepted that much of your compensation will be based on commissions and ever-changing compensation plans. If you want to keep earning more money, you must commit to getting feedback and an accurate depiction of your strengths and weaknesses.

> **If you want to keep earning more money, you must commit to getting feedback and an accurate depiction of your strengths and weaknesses.**

Now that we have explored all the benefits that can be obtained by implementing a win/loss analysis system, in the next two chapters we will review the reasons this can be a frustrating and complex problem for many salespeople that results in incomplete and/or inaccurate information.

CHAPTER SUMMARY

- Prospects share the complete truth with salespeople about why they lose a deal only 40 percent of the time. Therefore, in 60 percent of new business situations, salespeople do not have a complete and accurate understanding of why they lost.
- Ninety percent of salespeople believe they could improve upon how they debrief with prospects to get more candid feedback.

The Benefits of Postdecision Interviews

Postdecision interviews allow you to

- Develop your own organic self-improvement training program by applying feedback to your entire sales process.
- Implement tactics that are more effective and actionable than typical sales training.
- Take responsibility for the true, candid reasons prospects buy and don't buy from you/your company.
- Improve the effectiveness of your sales presentations and sales team.
- Determine key drivers for closing new business.
- Identify prospect perceptions of the strengths and weaknesses of your products and services.
- Formally share prospect perceptions with your organization to enhance product development.
- Uncover unmet prospect/customer needs.
- Benchmark and track your company's sales effectiveness against the competition and identify ways in which competitors are positioning themselves against you.

Understand the Postdecision Mind-Set of the Prospect

The next two chapters of this book will explore the reasons it can be difficult for you as a salesperson to fully and accurately understand why you win and lose in new business situations. This is an important next step because it is only after you fully understand the problem that you will be in the best position to develop and implement a solution.

So why is it that sales reps do not typically get the full truth from prospects about why they win and lose? Most salespeople simply blame prospects for not being truthful, potentially validating the old sales saying that "buyers are liars." Although this is true to some extent, prospects are only one half of the equation. What most salespeople don't fully understand is that sales reps also significantly contribute to this problem and are in many ways just as responsible for communication gaps that can occur.

In Chapters 2 and 3, we will explore the main areas that cause postdecision communication gaps. As Figure 2.1 shows, these areas include: (1) the reasons *prospects* are not candid during postdecision debriefs; (2) the ways in which *salespeople* inhibit the feedback process; and (3) overlapping areas of communication failure, whereby prospects and salespeople may both be at fault.

As a starting point, it's important to better understand the prospect mind-set during debriefs. This will enable you to more fully

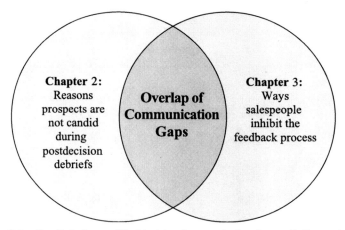

Figure 2.1   Two Main Areas of Postdecision Communication Gaps with Prospects

understand the communication barriers you face and better position your postdecision discussions to overcome them.

Let's review six reasons *prospects* are typically not candid in their feedback to salespeople once a deal has been won or lost.

1. PROSPECTS DO NOT WANT TO HURT THE SALESPERSON'S FEELINGS

The first and most intuitive reason prospects often deny you the truth is that many prospects simply feel uncomfortable giving critical and constructive feedback. Whether the feedback is about the sales process itself or your company's products and services, many prospects don't want to hurt your feelings, so what they do is provide feedback that is not entirely candid. This is human nature at its core. Not everyone has the ability to look at a situation critically, and some people don't possess the ability to be critical at all.

> Whether the feedback is about the sales process itself or your company's products and services, many prospects don't want to hurt your feelings, so what they do is provide feedback that is not entirely candid.

Additionally, prospects often feel they have already given you enough bad news because they did not give you their business. They are therefore reluctant to give you more negative information.

This problem is further exacerbated because prospects do not have the option of remaining anonymous on a feedback call with you. This is one reason some companies are no longer relying on their sales teams to conduct this research. Today, more and more companies are using independent interviewers from outside organizations, a process that allows prospects to remain anonymous and be more candid in their feedback.

To illustrate this point, let's consider the analogy of a couple breaking up. Often, one partner will not tell the other partner the true reasons the breakup occurred; however, that partner will speak very candidly about the situation to numerous third parties. People are more likely to tell a bartender their relationship problems than they are to tell their partners. This confrontation-avoiding behavior can best be summed up by the old saying, "It's not you, it's me."

When asked why prospects lack candor, most salespeople reply that prospects are uncomfortable because they don't want to hurt anyone's feelings. In fact, in a recent sales study of more than 500 salespeople, "prospects not wanting to hurt the sales rep's feelings" was the number one reason given by salespeople for postdecision communication gaps with prospects. If it is true that prospects do not want to hurt salespeople's feelings by giving feedback, then it must mean there are negative things that *could* be said to most sales reps. If salespeople intuitively feel that this is a main reason prospects are holding back, then salespeople themselves understand that there must be some things they could improve upon during the sales process.

Are you starting to see the challenge here? The problem is that this type of sometimes harsh feedback is exactly what you need to hear from prospects in order to do your job better. This is why you will need to counterbalance this prospect mind-set and change how each prospect views the feedback process. You will need to allay prospect fears by positioning them as trusted advisor/confidants and truly convincing them that you are looking for their help and honest criticism. In Part 2, we will cover more tactical steps to overcome this challenge.

> If it is true that prospects do not want to hurt salespeople's feelings by giving feedback, then it must mean there are negative things that *could* be said to most sales reps.

2. PROSPECTS FEAR CONFRONTATION

In many ways, salespeople are not naturally in an objective position to obtain the truth from prospects, and because of this, salespeople can often become defensive or may try to "resell" the prospect during the feedback call. This is a natural occurrence for some sales reps because they are trained to handle objections. When salespeople begin to hear the reasons they lost a deal, some try to reposition their product or service during the feedback conversation. Some sales reps can become frustrated during this type of dialogue because they might feel that one of the reasons given for losing was something they had already addressed and overcome.

This situation is complex because the salesperson is facing rejection, and let's face it, no one likes rejection. It is an unpleasant feeling, so it is human nature to put up defense mechanisms. When sales reps consciously or unconsciously become defensive in the midst of being rejected, prospects pick up on this and in turn can become less forthright because they simply don't want to get into an argument.

I'm sure that many of you reading this might be thinking, "I never do this on a feedback call." But the truth of the matter is, it doesn't matter whether you personally do this or not. The simple fact is that there are salespeople out there who handle these types of situations this way. I'm sure you may even know a couple of salespeople on your team or that you have met in your career who act like pit bulls and are pushy in their closing techniques. In many ways, these types of salespeople can intimidate prospects, and since many prospects have dealt with these types of high pressure sales tactics before, they have essentially been conditioned to avoid confrontation with salespeople (especially in a postdecision conversation). So even if you don't act this way, just remember that prospects will try to avoid confrontation or criticism from you during the feedback call, and because of this, they will often be less forthcoming and candid.

In other cases, rather than acting defensively or aggressively when receiving bad news, some salespeople tend to become subdued or deflated when a deal is lost. In these cases, prospects may try to cheer you up by sugarcoating the feedback if they sense that you feel deflated and rejected (particularly in situations where there is a long sales cycle and a meaningful relationship has been developed). Personal relationships can complicate the matter and compromise the feedback process.

This is one area where there is a lot of overlap of who is at fault, as both salespeople and prospects influence the outcome. In fact, often both sides play off each other during the conversation in a symbiotic way. How a salesperson acts on a feedback call will directly impact the type and depth of feedback a prospect is willing to provide.

Whether you become defensive, try to resell the prospect, or become deflated, just remember that your actions may be causing the prospect to be less forthcoming. You will need to neutralize these instincts if you wish to obtain more candor from prospects in the future. This is as much your problem to deal with as it is your prospects'.

3. PROSPECTS DON'T SPEND A LOT OF TIME GIVING SALESPEOPLE BAD NEWS

In *Rain Making*, Ford Harding (Avon, Mass.: Adams Media, 2008, pp. 254–264) highlights that another reason prospects are typically not forthcoming is because prospects usually do not want to spend a lot of time with salespeople when they need to tell them they lost a deal. As we covered in the previous two sections, giving a salesperson bad news is an uncomfortable process, and most prospects try to get it over with as quickly as possible. This is why you often feel rushed when a prospect is telling you that you lost the deal and is giving you the reasons for the loss.

Additionally, the prospect may need to make other calls to other salespeople to let them know they too lost the deal. In fact, the more salespeople (or companies) that are involved in a given sales process, the less likely the prospect will be to spend a meaningful amount of time debriefing with each salesperson. Although the prospect knows that it is necessary to make these calls, they are primarily a courtesy and not contributing to the prospect's responsibilities surrounding moving forward with the chosen firm. This sometimes leads to rushed interactions.

This is also why many times you will get the news about a lost deal by e-mail. Prospects are simply reluctant to tell salespeople that they lost a deal, and therefore they choose a more controlled environment in which to do so. Sometimes there is no way around this for a salesperson, as e-mail can be an effective way to follow up with a prospect about pending business. However, e-mail is not conducive to getting feedback on any sales situation because e-mail lacks context and emotion; it does not allow for a true dialogue or for any probing of meaningful and constructive criticism.

Prospects will also sometimes choose to leave you a voice mail regarding a lost sale. Some will even wait until after business hours to leave the message, and they will often give you a short synopsis about why you lost on the voice mail. As with an e-mail, prospects are often trying to avoid a longer, in depth conversation by leaving this after-hours voice mail.

I'm sure you've experienced these types of situations in which prospects try to keep things brief and simple or try to have it be a one-way dialogue over e-mail or voice mail. Just remember, in situations where prospects must give you bad news, they are likely to feel uncomfortable and will try to get you off the phone as soon as possible. Since they will try to rush through the reasons behind your losing the deal, the explanation they will give you will probably be brief and in many cases may not even be factual.

> In situations where prospects must give you bad news, they are likely to feel uncomfortable and will try to get you off the phone as soon as possible.

As we will explore in Part 2 of the book, this is why the feedback process must be slowed down to allow for a more detailed critique. The way to do this is to acquiesce to the prospect's mind-set by graciously accepting the news and allowing the prospect to disengage from the call quickly, while at the same time setting up a separate and distinct call with the prospect for the purpose of gathering more detailed feedback.

4. EARLIER PROBLEMS IN THE SALES PROCESS CAN IMPACT PROSPECT CANDOR

Another reason prospects may not be fully candid is that they may have had issues with you as the sales rep or your company's sales process and therefore may be particularly sensitive to giving you critical feedback. In fact, in an average win/loss analysis program (when conducted by an independent third party), 38 percent of prospects cite sales problems or issues as a deciding factor in losing a deal. Additionally, in 21 percent of bids won situations, prospects cite issues with the sales rep/sales process even though they awarded their business to the sales rep.

Several common negative sales behaviors contribute to these percentages, with the most frequent being a failure on behalf of the salesperson to

> **Thirty-eight percent of prospects cite sales problems or issues as a deciding factor in losing a deal.**

understand and address the prospect's unique needs. Figure 2.2 highlights other commonly mentioned sales issues, including not treating prospects as important, ineffective sales presentations, a lack of chemistry with the prospect/cultural fit with the prospect's organization, and team selling/complex sales issues. We will explore each of these issues in more detail in Chapter 7.

Figure 2.2 links up well with the statistic that highlights the fact that 32 percent of the time, sales reps are totally wrong in their assessment for losing. Since we know that for a typical sales team, prospects will have issues with the salesperson or sales process and presentation 38 percent of the time, it stands to reason that in many of these cases, prospects will simply not provide this feedback to sales reps. This situation poses a major problem for salespeople because this is exactly the type of feedback that can be used to improve future sales performance.

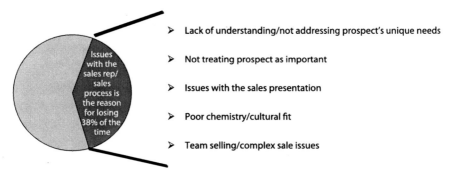

Figure 2.2   Most Frequently Mentioned Issues with the Sales Process

To illustrate this point, ask yourself, if you were going through a buying process and you felt that the sales rep did a poor job, was not articulate, or delivered a poor presentation, would you be willing to give them candid feedback? My guess is many people would be unwilling to do so initially and instead may blame something else for why they did not choose to do business with them. It is simply an uncomfortable situation.

Some of you may be thinking, "Yes, I would be willing to give candid feedback to a sales rep." But here is the problem: you must remember that you are a salesperson, and salespeople look at this situation differently from people who are not in sales. For example, you know how hard it is to get up every day and sell for a living. Therefore, you are more likely to want to help out other salespeople and give them the information they need to be successful. This is because you have been in their shoes. This is why I have often found it easier to sell to salespeople because they are generally more open and honest with me, and they tend to not waste my time.

So, in an effort to neutralize your bias as a salesperson and give you better insight into the prospect's mind-set, suppose you went to a play or to see a musical group perform and you did not enjoy the show. If asked, would you be willing to tell the performers that you thought they did a poor job and list the areas they could improve upon during their performance? My guess is that many of you would be less than completely honest because you would not want to hurt their feelings. That said, if you were able to give them feedback without the fear of hurting their feelings, you could help them be more successful in future performances.

So now you have a more calibrated view of your prospect's mind-set. Just as you would not want to give critical feedback to an actor or musician, prospects often choose not to give critical feedback to you on your sales performance.

This is perhaps the largest stumbling block for most salespeople to get around during the postdecision debrief process. Many salespeople are not sure how they can improve their selling efforts and often throw up their hands and blame it on the fact that prospects are not forthcoming. In fact, it is somewhat rare that I hear salespeople talk about what they themselves can do better during the sales process (of course, when we win, we all do take credit for our sales successes). Instead, salespeople often tend to blame some types of product or pricing deficiency as the reasons they lose deals, or else simply blame it on the "unreasonable" prospects.

In fact, when more than 500 salespeople were asked what percent of the time they believed they were at fault for losing deals, the average salesperson believed that his or her personal performance was to blame only 25 percent of the time. But let's not stop there: interestingly, salespeople on average believe that 75 percent of the time, they are a major reason a deal is won. I found both of these statistics very telling. How could the average salesperson believe that he is at fault for losing only 25 percent of the time, but believe that he is the primary reason for winning deals 75 percent of the time? Doesn't this seem like a disconnect to you?

These statistics prove that salespeople overemphasize their impact on why deals are won and underemphasize their impact on why deals are lost. Now, I understand we all need strong egos to overcome the daily rejection of being in sales, but this is taking it a bit far.

In some ways, this disconnect is not entirely the salesperson's fault. Over the years, a typical salesperson may have become conditioned by prospects giving incomplete information about wins and losses. If most salespeople are getting inaccurate information about why they lose, which is typically more skewed toward product or pricing deficiencies, over time, salespeople begin to believe that those are the only true issues.

The bottom line is that salespeople are instrumental in why deals are won and lost, and because of this, prospects often have a hard time giving constructive criticism directly to salespeople. As Figure 2.3 shows, whether a deal is won or lost, salespeople typically have an impact on the outcome about 40 percent of the time.

> Salespeople overemphasize their impact on why deals are won and underemphasize their impact on why deals are lost.

Therefore, in about 40 percent of new business situations, whether a salesperson wins or loses, it is a direct result of the salesperson's own performance during the sales process. This data comes from thousands of independent, in-depth interviews conducted by highly

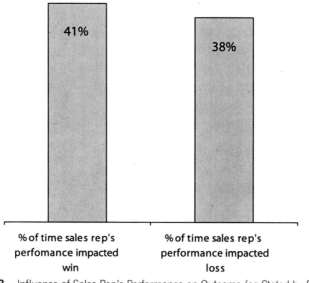

Figure 2.3   Influence of Sales Rep's Performance on Outcome (as Stated by Prospects)

trained interviewers. So if we compare this information to salespeople's own perceptions, you can see that salespeople are underemphasizing how often they impact a loss (on average, prospects cite that sales reps are a main reason for losing 38 percent of the time versus 25 percent stated by sales reps) and overemphasizing how often they impact a win (on average, 41 percent of prospects cite that sales reps impact a win versus 75 percent stated by sales reps).

> Whether a deal is won or lost, salespeople typically have an impact on the outcome of a deal about 40 percent of the time.

Let's take this one step further. As Figure 2.4 shows, in 23 percent of new business situations, salespeople win or lose despite their own performance. To clarify, what this means is that when a salesperson wins a deal, he or she frequently wins despite a weak sales performance. In other words, the prospect had issues with the sales rep or sales process yet still chose to buy from the salesperson despite these issues.

This also happens during bids lost situations whereby the salesperson can do a great job (and be cited as a strength during the sales process), but the prospect still chooses to go with another company/salesperson.

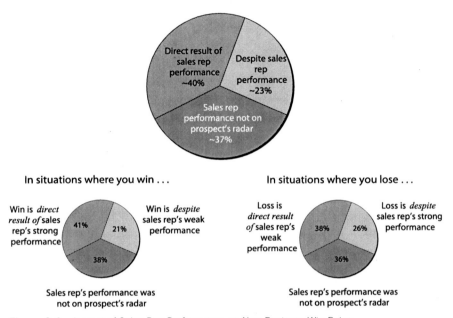

In situations where you win . . .   In situations where you lose . . .

Figure 2.4   Impact of Sales Rep Performance on New Business Win Rates

If we add the 23 percent of situations where sales reps win or lose despite their own performance together with the 40 percent of situations where their performance resulted in a win or loss, you are looking at 63 percent of new business situations where salespeople have an impact on the prospects (i.e., the sales reps influenced the prospects enough to be mentioned as one of the top strengths or weaknesses). Not surprisingly, salespeople have a direct impact on how much business is won (and lost).

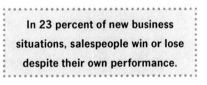

In 23 percent of new business situations, salespeople win or lose despite their own performance.

One final note on Figure 2.4: on average, 37 percent of the time the salesperson is not cited as impacting the deal at all. This means that either the prospect was not basing her decision on the salesperson's performance or simply that the salesperson was not able to make an impact either way.

All of this information should help you as a salesperson realize that the less competitive elements of your sales performance are often a deciding factor, and because of this, prospects may choose to be less forthcoming with you during a postdecision debrief.

5. THE REAL REASONS FOR LOSS MAY MAKE THE PROSPECT LOOK BAD

Another reason for limited candor from prospects could be that they do not want to share the real reasons with you because it would make them look bad (for instance, if the decision maker chose a friend for the business or made a decision that was for selfish reasons rather than for the good of the business).

Another particularly unsettling reason prospects may not be totally forthcoming is that they themselves may not be 100 percent sure of why you did not get the business. This could be because the prospect was not as involved in the decision-making process as you initially thought. Or perhaps a last minute decision was made by people more senior to the prospect, and therefore the prospect was not privy to the real reasons. In any of these scenarios, prospects will be less forthcoming with you because they will not want to admit their own lack of understanding or decision-making authority.

Additionally, there will always be certain sales situations where you have been invited into the sales process simply to compare or verify a decision to buy from another company/salesperson. Often, buyers can be commissioned (by more senior persons within their organizations) with the task of getting quotes or bids from three or more vendors. In these situations, buyers will often have already made their decision and are just using you to make them feel better about their decision and/or to be able to bargain better with their chosen company.

We've all been in this position at some point in our sales careers, and this is a fact of life; however, once you learn how to better conduct your own win/loss analysis on yourself, over time you will learn how to better spot these situations and can ultimately spend less time and emotional energy on these types of prospects.

In situations where you are in the deal merely for the purposes of the prospect's negotiation with the winning vendor, the prospect will rarely tell you the true reasons for why you lost the business because it will make him look bad and may open him up to criticism. Therefore, the best way to solve this problem is to learn how to de-sell or disengage from these prospects as quickly as possible. We will cover these sales techniques in more detail in Chapter 8.

Obviously, these are frustrating situations for all salespeople. However, it is important to realize that in some cases, prospects will be less forthcoming because they do not want to look bad.

6. RELUCTANCE TO SHARE INFORMATION ON THEIR CHOSEN VENDOR

Once prospects have gone through the buying process and have reviewed multiple products and services, they are in a unique position to speak candidly about the marketplace and other competitors. This situation represents a massive opportunity for salespeople to gather not only feedback about prospects' perceptions of their company, but also perceptions of competitors.

However, some prospects may be unwilling to provide competitive intelligence from one company directly to another. Some prospects may feel a sense of allegiance to the company they chose or might feel it would not be fair to tell one competitor about another.

Since some bids lost prospects can feel uncomfortable giving out competitive information to sales reps, it can leave a significant portion of the reason for the loss unexplained. Additionally, sales reps may choose not to ask prospects about competitors because they don't want to put the prospects in an awkward position. This is yet another reason prospects may be less forthcoming and candid during a bids lost postdecision debrief, and if salespeople shy away from asking detailed questions about the competition, this again can be an area of overlap with respect to who is causing the communication gap.

As we will show later, this is why speaking with bids won customers can be a valuable tool for gathering competitive intelligence. Bids won customers will be more likely to provide you with valuable insights because you are now, in a sense, on the same team.

CHAPTER WRAP-UP

As we've covered, prospects often feel uncomfortable giving you direct feedback or criticism because they don't want to hurt your feelings or they may be afraid of confrontation. Combine this with the fact that prospects don't want to spend a lot of time giving you bad news about a loss or they do not want to look bad, and you can start to see how this area of the sales process can become problematic and often ends up with you scratching your head in confusion about why you lost the deal.

This has always been one of the more frustrating parts of being in sales. When you don't fully understand why you lose, you will often spend an inordinate amount of time reflecting on what went wrong. When you add up all the time you spend trying to figure out why you lose, you can begin to see how getting better information from prospects would not only save you time but make you more effective.

All of the reasons for prospects not being candid that we reviewed in this chapter add up and can inhibit the postdecision debrief process. Additionally, prospects can often have multiple reasons for not being forthcoming, so you may need to overcome a variety of issues in order to get the full truth. The most important point is that these issues can cause any true and candid feedback to come through in a disproportionate way. The moment a prospect omits an important portion of the true reasons for a loss, it automatically compromises the rest of the feedback. Without all the elements of the loss understood, it is impossible to accurately and proportionally assess the loss. It then also becomes difficult for you to make the appropriate enhancements to your sales process.

Although these issues may seem insurmountable, there are several ways to address them, which we will explore in Part 2. For now, what is most important is that you have a better understanding of all of these issues. This is an important step so that you can start recognizing them in order to ultimately overcome them.

Now that we have explored all the reasons surrounding prospects' reluctance to be candid during postdecision debriefs, let's review how you as a salesperson may be further inhibiting the feedback process.

CHAPTER SUMMARY

Reasons for Prospects Not Being Forthcoming and Candid

- Prospects often feel uncomfortable giving feedback and criticism directly to salespeople because they do not want to hurt their feelings.
- Prospects often fear confrontation or criticism from sales reps who can become defensive while receiving feedback.
- Prospects don't spend a lot of time giving salespeople bad news.
- Prospects often have issues with the sales reps or sales process that can impact their candor.
- The real reasons for loss may make the prospect look bad.
- Prospects may feel reluctant to provide too much information on their chosen vendors.

Sales Statistics

- Whether a deal is won or lost, prospects indicate that salespeople typically have an impact on the outcome of a deal about 40 percent of the time.
- In 23 percent of new business situations, salespeople win or lose despite their own performance.
- Salespeople believe they are at fault for losing only 25 percent of the time but believe they are the primary reason for winning deals 75 percent of the time. Therefore, salespeople overestimate themselves as a factor in winning and underestimate themselves as a reason for losing.

Recognize How Salespeople Can Inhibit the Feedback Process

As we explored in Chapter 2, there are many ways in which prospects inhibit the flow of accurate and candid information during postdecision debriefs. Each of these reasons is important and should not be overlooked. However, there are also many ways in which salespeople themselves inhibit the candor of the debrief process.

This chapter is especially important as I will walk through how *you* may be inhibiting the flow of accurate information. There will always be prospect factors that may be outside of your direct control, but what you can control is your approach to the situation.

Let's review six ways salespeople "get in their own way" when they debrief with prospects.

1. SALESPEOPLE ARE NOT IN AN OBJECTIVE POSITION TO OBTAIN UNBIASED FEEDBACK

The first reason salespeople are typically unable to capture accurate reasons for losing is that they are not in an objective position to receive and interpret feedback. Some of the reasons it may be difficult for you to remain objective during a postdecision debrief include the following:

* *Bias and perceptions.* Sales reps naturally have their own biases and perceptions of the sales process and of the prospects, which

can act as a filter to the truth. In many cases, salespeople are too close to the sales process, and this can cloud their ability to accept or understand candid feedback. Even in situations where prospects are giving candid feedback, salespeople may misinterpret what they're saying or may find themselves selectively listening.

- *Lack of chemistry with the prospect.* Many times you will lose a deal because the prospect did not believe you were a good fit or did not feel chemistry with you. We all "click" with certain types of people better than others. We see this in everyday life; we simply don't get along with everybody. Instead, we become friends with, work with, and buy from a select group of people who we feel share the same values as we do.

  This is no different during the sales process. When a salesperson has lost a deal, it often means that he or she didn't "click" as well with the prospect in comparison to the winning sales rep. Therefore, prospects will be less forthcoming with someone to whom they do not feel as connected. If the salesperson doesn't connect well with the prospect, it is unlikely that he or she will be able to fully understand the prospect's viewpoint. This does not mean that the prospect's feedback is any less valuable; in fact, it may be more valuable to you as a salesperson.

- *Inaccuracy of assessment of prospect's needs.* Often, the reason for loss has to do with the salesperson's inability to accurately assess the prospect's needs and focus on hot button issues. In many cases, the true reason for a loss is that you as the salesperson could not accurately determine what the prospect was looking for in the first place. Therefore, your entire sales pitch and presentation may have been based on incorrect conclusions. If a sales rep loses a deal because she didn't correctly understand what the prospect was looking for in the first place, she will most likely not understand this at the end of the process either. The sales rep may simply have blinders on.

- *Fear of accountability.* Some sales reps may not want to gather the truth because they do not want to be held accountable. If a sales rep feels responsible for losing a deal, he or she may choose to limit the amount of feedback gathered.

> * *Hesitancy to reach out to prospect after a loss.* Some salespeople fear bothering prospects when conducting postdecision debrief calls, or they may feel bad about losing in the first place so they don't want to face the lost prospects again. Sales requires a lot of persistence and repeat calls to prospects. Many salespeople hesitate in calling prospects one more time for a debrief. Many salespeople assume they will be better off moving on to the next deal versus tracking down the prospect and gathering this information. The fact that salespeople feel they would be bothering prospects may partially explain why salespeople conduct loss reviews only 45 percent of the time.

It's a tough spot to be in as a salesperson when you are trying to gather your own feedback. You are not in an objective position, so you must learn how to counteract this problem through such tactics as notifying prospects early in the sales cycle that you will be reaching out to them postdecision (whether you win or lose) to garner their feedback, or using someone else to conduct the interviews on your behalf.

2. SALESPEOPLE ARE OFTEN UNPREPARED WHEN CONDUCTING A DEBRIEF

Salespeople can often be caught off guard by the prospect's bad news about a lost deal. When a prospect calls a sales rep to tell him that he didn't get the business, most times the sales rep will immediately ask why the deal was lost. Only 19 percent of salespeople set up separate calls to perform a postdecision debrief with prospects. This means that most salespeople are conducting their debriefs on the same call when

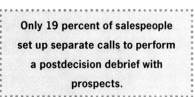

Only 19 percent of salespeople set up separate calls to perform a postdecision debrief with prospects.

they receive the bad news from the prospect. As I will show in Part 2, the best way to get candid and thorough feedback is by setting up a separate call with the prospect (preferably at a later date when you have put the loss behind you).

> **When salespeople attempt to debrief with prospects on the same calls as when the prospects are notifying them about lost deals, sales reps are often not fully prepared with their lines of questioning.**

When salespeople attempt to debrief with prospects on the same calls as when the prospects are notifying them about lost deals, sales reps are often not fully prepared with their lines of questioning. It is hard for salespeople to gather all the information they need when they are asking questions on the spur of the moment. As a result, some areas of the sales process may not be covered simply because the sales rep was not prepared during the feedback session.

This situation causes a lot of challenges for salespeople. As we explored in Chapter 2, prospects do not like to spend a lot of time with you when they are telling you that you did not get their business. Their mind-set is one in which they are trying to get you off the phone as soon as possible. Combine this with the fact that the salesperson can be caught off guard and unprepared to conduct a debrief, and you often get a rushed conversation that allows for little probing and little factual and detailed information. Yet this is what most salespeople do; they try to get feedback on the same call as when they hear the news about a loss and face the previously mentioned obstacles. The "breakup" call is perhaps the *worst* time for the salesperson to gather feedback.

Another challenge is that the sales rep may be so shocked by the loss that he may not initially accept it as a loss. In sales situations where the shock of a loss hasn't had time to sink in, aggressive selling (by either the sales reps themselves or their managers who are now also working on new information) may lead to alienation. This alienation may inhibit the ability to gain objective feedback later.

> **The "breakup" call is perhaps the *worst* time for the salesperson to gather feedback.**

Worse, it may also close the door on future sales opportunities based on the negative impression that is left behind with the prospect.

All of these reasons are why slowing down the debrief process and setting up a second call is so valuable.

3. SALESPEOPLE USUALLY DO NOT KNOW THE RIGHT QUESTIONS TO ASK (AND HOW TO ASK THEM)

Perhaps the biggest reason sales reps typically don't get the true reasons for a loss is that most salespeople do not know the right questions to ask and, perhaps more importantly, how to ask them. Most sales training focuses only on situations during the sales process rather than on postsales etiquette.

Why is it that most salespeople have never learned how to conduct this process in a more productive and useful manner?

- *Limited research and literature.* Much has been written and studied on all of the other elements within the sales process, but little has been covered on the postdecision debrief process. Historically, there has been very little research and therefore very little written on the subject matter of postdecision debriefs and win/loss analysis. For instance, very few sales books address the topic of postdecision debriefs, and those that do typically provide less than a few pages on the subject. Additionally, there have been very few articles published on this topic.

  > Much has been written and studied on all of the other elements within the sales process, but little has been covered on the postdecision debrief process.

- *Sales training programs/seminars generally do not cover win/loss reviews.* Sales training and sales seminars also rarely cover how to appropriately conduct postdecision debriefs and the benefits of the process. Many salespeople listen to audio programs in their cars to increase their knowledge of the sales process and to inspire them to win more business, and these programs have also left this important topic uncovered.

- *Sales managers often overlook this key aspect of the sales process.* Since there has been little in the way of sales literature and training on this subject matter, most sales managers overlook this valuable tool. With limited emphasis from sales management and senior management within sales organizations, most salespeople continue to perform win/loss reviews in sporadic and unproductive ways. However, do not let this fool you. Every sales manager and head of sales asks her salespeople why they win and lose deals, although most typically accept mere anecdotal answers from their sales teams.

Often my company receives a call from a head of sales or head of marketing after a meeting in which no sales team member around the conference room table was able to explain why he was winning or losing. My company is hired as an independent third party firm to perform this work and to implement a formal program.

Although most companies have not historically had formal programs in place that gauge why they win and lose business, this situation is changing. In fact, over the last 15 years, more and more companies have been hiring outside third parties to implement win/loss analysis programs. By using an independent, outside party to interview prospects after buying decisions have been made, sales teams and companies can learn the true, candid reasons why they win and lose. However, at present, only 18 percent of salespeople indicate that they have been involved in a formal win/loss program, which suggests that there is still a significant number of companies that are missing out on the immense benefits gained through this unique management tool.

> Only 18 percent of salespeople indicate that they have been involved in a formal win/loss program.

All of these reasons compound upon the issues we explored in the last chapter. As we've shown, getting candid feedback from prospects postdecision is already a challenging process to begin with. When you add in the fact that there has been little research, training, and focus from corporate senior management, you can start to see why it is so hard for salespeople to learn the best tactics and understand the right questions to ask (and how to ask them).

4. SALESPEOPLE TYPICALLY DO NOT DEBRIEF WITH BIDS WON PROSPECTS

While most of this chapter has focused on ways in which salespeople inhibit the feedback process for lost deals, it's important to note that salespeople don't often learn why they *win*, either. The average sales rep asks customers why they won only 40 percent of the time. Most of the time, salespeople are elated that they won the business and simply move on to the next deal.

Researching wins as well as losses ensures that you receive a balanced perspective so that you can continue the practices that result in success and

> **The average sales rep asks customers why they won only 40 percent of the time.**

learn what is important to procure business. Also remember, our research showed that sometimes sales reps win despite mixed perceptions of their ability from prospects surveyed. Even when you win, objective feedback helps balance the "thrill of the win" with objective reality that will help propel you toward your next win.

Interviewing prospects who choose to work with you is valuable because these prospects will often be very candid about their reasons for giving you their business, as well as giving you feedback on any areas where you might improve your salesmanship or products and services. In contrast to bids lost prospects, bids won prospects are often very willing to tell you what they think about you as a sales professional, your company's products and services, and the competition.

There are many reasons why bids won prospects are more forthcoming with both positive and negative information:

* *Bids won prospects like to talk about their decisions because it makes them feel good.* It also helps them to justify to themselves that they made the right choice. By explaining to you all the reasons they chose you and your firm, they are validating their decision-making process. Have you ever noticed that once you make a decision, you feel a sense of relief and like to talk about the choice you made with other people?
* *Bids won prospects also like to talk to you about why they chose you because it helps them with the transition between the sales process and customer service.* Once prospects choose a particular company, they sometimes feel a sense of buyer's remorse whereby they feel good about their choice but then can feel a drop-off as they transition into the company's existing service

structure. Some prospects/new customers are unhappy when they lose their salesperson as their primary point of contact. They had developed a relationship with the sales rep, and now that relationship is gone or needs to be rebuilt with others in the company. The actual process of reaching out to your new customers and debriefing with them can be very therapeutic and allows you to end your sales cycle with the prospect feeling good. This also allows prospects to ask you any questions they may have about the relationship with your company moving forward.

* ***Bids won prospects are more apt to like you personally.*** The prospects likely "clicked" with you (or they felt they fit well with your organization), and because they like you, they will probably feel more comfortable with you. As a result, they can be more forthcoming with both positive and negative feedback.

* ***Prospects who choose to work with your firm are now, in a sense, on your team and are more invested in the relationship.*** New customers become part of your organization and therefore have a sense of allegiance and a vested interest. You are now playing on the same team, so any feedback they give you will help them in the future, as well. For example, if a bid won prospect saw other interesting products or features at another competitor that your company does not provide, she will likely be willing to share this information with you because she has an interest in your company eventually providing these same services or features to her.

* ***Bids won prospects will also be willing to share salesmanship feedback with you because they chose you and therefore will be less likely to feel that they are hurting your feelings.*** As I showed in the last chapter, 21 percent of bids won prospects cite salesmanship issues during debriefs. Therefore, there is a lot of constructive feedback and information that can be gleaned from bids won prospects. Even though they chose you, they still might have valuable feedback, and they won't feel as bad giving it to you because you still got the business (and your commission check!). Bids won prospects simply feel more comfortable sharing negative feedback because they don't have

to worry as much about hurting your feelings. Also, because they selected you, they can use the sandwich method of giving feedback whereby they will tell you all your strengths, then share some negative feedback, then finish up with more positive. This is much easier to do with the salesperson to whom they awarded the business.

Debriefing with sold customers who chose to work with you and your company is a valuable yet often overlooked exercise. When you interview bids won prospects, you will learn about what your greatest strengths

> Debriefing with sold customers who chose to work with you and your company is a valuable yet often overlooked exercise.

are in the eyes of your prospects. This will allow you to promote you and your company's positive qualities over time. You can also garner valuable feedback about areas for improvement.

It is always important to understand why you win because this information acts as a powerful complement to the reasons you lose. In fact, if you focus only on why you lose and don't understand why you win, it will be difficult to truly understand and utilize your full salesmanship toolkit. Learning why you win will give you a clearer perspective on why you lose.

5. THE TRUE REASONS FOR LOSS ARE DIFFICULT TO OBTAIN IF YOU ARE NOT SELLING DIRECTLY TO THE DECISION MAKER

Another reason you may not be able to accurately assess why you are winning and losing is that you might be selling to the wrong person in the first place (i.e., you may be selling to a contact at the wrong organizational level). This is why it is so important to sell to the top and to start your sales process with a senior-level decision maker. When you begin your sales dialogue with the actual decision maker, you will find that you have a much smoother sales process and, ultimately, debrief process.

In contrast, when you begin your sales cycle with someone who is not the final decision maker, you will have to work your way up the organizational ladder to ultimately get to the end decision maker. These types of prospects are commonly referred to as "champions" or "key influencers" and can be a great source of information that can be very helpful when you do finally meet with the end decision maker. However, this can be a time consuming and tedious process and can limit not only your closing ratio but also your ability to truly understand why you win and lose. It can also severely lengthen your sales process and cause you to spend a lot more time and money selling each deal.

> When you begin your sales dialogue with the actual decision maker, you will find that you have a much smoother sales process and, ultimately, debrief process.

Here are three main challenges you will face in situations where you are not selling directly to the decision maker:

- *Your prospect may not have enough influence within his organization.* It will always be difficult for you to know if you are getting the most accurate information from your prospect when you are not dealing with the final decision maker because it will be tough to tell how much influence this particular person actually has within your target company. For example, your prospect may not be respected in the organization, so even if you sell him on the idea, your products and services might be tainted because you are being presented internally through the lens of someone who may not have enough influence or political clout to get you to the next level of decision making. You may not win the business because the actual decision maker does not get along with your contact and therefore minimizes whatever initiatives this person brings to the table. In this situation, your contact will never tell you that you didn't get the business because he simply did not have enough political capital or goodwill to get it done. Believe me, no prospect will ever tell you that; he might not even know it.
- *Your prospect may not be very good at sales/selling ideas.* When you begin your sales process at the wrong level, you will often need to have your initial prospect go to bat for you to get future sales meetings set up, information, or decisions made,

and so on. The problem you have in this scenario is that you will only be as good as your initial prospect's own sales skills, and let's face it: no one can sell your product as well as you. Therefore, if your initial prospect does not possess strong selling skills or is not decisive, you will be in a position whereby someone else is selling for you and is not very good at it, a precarious situation. This does not just have to do with salesmanship; it could also be that your initial prospect may not have strong communication skills and therefore may be less able to steer you in the right direction and/or communicate to you why you won or lost the business.

* ***Your prospect may not be senior enough to understand the true needs of her organization.*** When you don't sell to the end decision maker, your prospect may also not be privy to all of the true needs for your products or services within her organization, and it will be very difficult for you to assess how to customize your presentation and sales process. You may lose the deal because you didn't have enough solid information to sell effectively. Your initial prospect may also reject your products and services even though her company really needs them.

This is a terrible place to be because once you have been boxed out by your initial prospect, your hands are tied. You will need to make a tough decision as to whether or not you will go over this person's head to get to the real decision maker.

My research does not suggest that you should ignore key influencers in the sales process and, naturally, their input and affirmation will be critical in a win. However, it does emphasize that a sales rep's business case must be strong enough (and he or she must also be confident enough) to be able to gain access to those individuals who are ultimately holding the purse strings. Sometimes selling to a key influencer can be your only way in the door, and often decision makers delegate the information gathering to someone else within their organizations, so many times you have no choice. All of the above factors point to why it is so critical to sell at the top when you can. Not only will your sales process be quicker and more efficient, but you will get more accurate and unfiltered information about why you win and lose (and where you are in the process) from the final decision maker.

If you lose a sale without ever meeting the decision maker, you have to take responsibility for this situation. The truth of the matter is that any feedback you get from your champion prospect (either positive or negative) will be compromised. If you never met with the decision maker and someone else presented your product or service for you, then you lost the deal because you yourself did not get to the right person. I know this may be hard for some of you to believe, but it is the truth. You must take responsibility and learn from these situations, and the main lesson is that when you don't get in front of the decision maker, that alone is the reason you lost, and that is your responsibility, not your prospect's responsibility.

> If you lose a sale without ever meeting the decision maker, you have to take responsibility for this situation.

Both prospects and salespeople contribute to the problem of gathering accurate and candid postdecision debrief information. Before we move on to exploring ways to solve these issues, let's review one last significant sales process scenario that often negatively impacts the ability of salespeople to understand why they win or lose: selling through intermediaries, channels, and partners.

Please note, if you are a direct sold salesperson (which means that you sell directly to your end user/prospect) and there is no third party involved in your sales process, you can skip to the end of this chapter.

6. INHERENT ISSUES WITH SELLING THROUGH INTERMEDIARIES, CHANNELS, AND PARTNERS

Although there are many variations to the sales process, one common sales approach involves selling through intermediaries, channels, or partners, whereby a third party develops a relationship with the prospect and then makes a sales presentation jointly with a product specialist or wholesaler. In fact, 40 percent of salespeople sell through some form of intermediary. This situation commonly occurs when a product or service is sold by a "generalist" who needs to bring in a "specialist" to sell the deal. The generalist would be the intermediary, and the specialist would be the salesperson.

For example, in the retirement services industry, 401(k) plans are now mostly sold through financial advisors, insurance brokers, payroll specialists, third-party administrators, registered investment advisors, or consultants (all generalists), and these types of intermediaries often bring in 401(k) wholesalers (also known as

> **Forty percent of salespeople sell through some form of intermediary.**

product specialists) to perform more detailed sales meetings and presentations with prospects.

This type of situation has become prevalent in many areas of the financial services industry such as custody, investment management, disability insurance, etc. It also exists in the technology and software arena where technology firms sell through channels and partners (a situation that will become more prevalent as globalization continues).

When salespeople (or wholesalers/product specialists) sell through intermediaries, it can often be difficult to have direct contact with the end prospect both during and after the sales process. Therefore, it can be challenging for salespeople to gather meaningful postdecision feedback from prospects simply because they have no direct relationship with them.

The problem for salespeople (or wholesalers) in these situations is that often the intermediary controls the sales process and maintains most of the contact with the end prospect. It can be difficult for the salesperson to conduct any type of debrief at all. Many times the wholesaler will not be allowed to contact the prospect because the intermediary controls the process. That means the salesperson typically hears any postdecision prospect feedback from an intermediary, channel, or partner secondhand, and since the intermediary controls the process, he also often controls what prospect feedback gets passed on to the salesperson.

Some feedback might also be thirdhand. This can occur in situations where the intermediary gets feedback from someone other than the true decision maker. For example, the intermediary gets the reasons for loss from someone who was involved in the decision

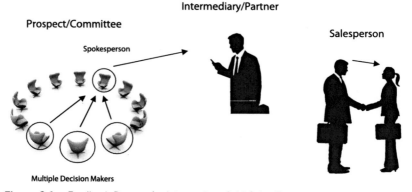

Figure 3.1 Feedback Process for Intermediary-Sold Sales Process

making/committee but who was not the primary decision maker. As Figure 3.1 shows, in this situation any feedback the salesperson gets will be thirdhand and will have already gone through each person's own "filter" before it reaches the end salesperson.

The problem with this type of communication pattern is analogous to the telephone whisper game that is often played by children. In the game, the first player whispers a phrase or sentence to the next player. Each player successively whispers what that player believes he or she heard to the next. The last player announces the statement to the entire group. Errors typically accumulate in the retellings. This game can be used as a business metaphor for cumulative error—especially as inaccurate information spreads—or, more generally, for the unreliability of human recollection. This metaphor points out the fact that inevitably, by the time prospect feedback makes its way through a committee and an intermediary, the message is watered down and is often quite different from what the prospect initially relayed.

Additionally, in some cases, intermediaries might be responsible for bringing several different salespeople (or vendors) to the table for the prospect. Often the intermediary will then be responsible for letting each wholesaler know why he won or lost the business. Since the intermediary might have to do multiple "bad news" calls with each finalist or wholesaler, it can often limit the amount of feedback the intermediary is willing to provide, similar to the prospect situation we discussed in Chapter 2.

There are many other problems with this scenario that can inhibit the flow of high-quality feedback from prospects. For one, because the salesperson has to rely on the intermediary for the postdecision feedback, she will always be at the mercy of how good or bad the intermediary is at gathering prospect commentary. As we've shown, most salespeople are not particularly educated at debriefing with prospects, and intermediaries are no different. Therefore, the information will be only as good as the intermediary who gathers and remembers all the specifics of the feedback from the prospect. Remember, because this is happening secondhand, a lot of the specifics and color can get lost in the translation to you as the end salesperson. This is especially prevalent when the intermediary might have his own agenda that may skew the feedback that eventually reaches the salesperson.

Additionally, many of the issues we explored in Chapter 2 apply in this situation. For example, there may be many reasons the intermediary might not tell you the full and honest truth. The intermediary might have been bringing you in and never intended to steer the business in your direction (for example, the intermediary might need to bring three parties to the table in order to show that he's doing his job). Or perhaps the intermediary really doesn't know why you lost and didn't bother to probe enough to get you actionable feedback and therefore will keep things brief and not give you the accurate truth. Or the intermediary may not want to give negative feedback because he does not want to hurt your feelings and knows that he will probably need to work with you again in future sales situations, and he does not want to jeopardize the long-term relationship. These are all reasons it can be tougher to get honest feedback from an intermediary, but obviously this depends on the intermediary; some will be more willing than others to let you know what you can do to improve.

Gathering feedback from an intermediary on a particular sales situation can be challenging, especially since this type of selling often results in a sales process that can come across as disjointed to the end prospect. In fact, results from more than 2,000 postsales process interviews conducted with prospects and intermediaries reveal two common (and related) issues with this type of sales approach:

1. Due to the nature of the intermediary-sold sales process, sales reps often have little time to build rapport with prospects. As a result, sales reps have difficulty assessing prospects' true needs both before and during sales meetings.
2. Prospects often cite a lack of chemistry or fit with specialist sales reps. They also often indicate that the sales reps do not fully understand their unique needs and therefore do not adequately customize the presentation.

Although the above themes are clearly sales issues, they are also the result of the fragmented nature of the intermediary-sold sales process itself. To illustrate the systemic issue at hand, let's take a step back and break down the entire sales process in more procedural terms.

There has been much research and writing on how the sales process can be broken down into different steps. For the purposes of this book, I am going to use and expand upon a seven phase sales process (see Figure 3.2): (1) Getting in the door, (2) establishing a connection/building rapport, (3) conducting a needs analysis, (4) presenting, (5) answering questions and handling objections, (6) closing the deal, and (7) debriefing with prospects.

As Figure 3.2 illustrates, when the sales process involves an intermediary, the key areas of the sales process are the same but are often fragmented due to the fact that the sales process is conducted jointly by the intermediary and the wholesaler/specialist. In many cases,

Figure 3.2   The Seven Elements of the Sales Process

intermediaries handle steps 1 through 3 (intermediaries do most of the prospecting, establishing a connection, and identifying the needs of the prospect). Wholesalers/product specialist sales reps then handle steps 4 and 5 as they present their capabilities, answer questions, and handle objections. Then the process typically shifts back to the intermediary to close the sale.

Intermediary-sold business, then, often results in a disjointed sales process as the management of the steps is shared between the intermediary and the sales rep. The problem with this approach is that wholesalers are often asked to present solutions with little time to build rapport and fully understand prospects' needs, leading to presentations that may lack understanding, insight, and customization. Clearly, there can be considerable upside to selling through intermediaries, and the pros far outweigh the cons, but sales reps need to make every effort to overcome the types of issues that arise from this splintered sales approach if they are to create a more seamless sales presentation for prospects.

> When the sales process involves an intermediary, the key areas of the sales process are the same but are often fragmented due to the fact that the sales process is conducted jointly by the intermediary and the wholesaler/specialist.

Selling through an intermediary, channel, or partner can severely limit a salesperson's ability to understand why she wins and loses in new business situations. This is why, when possible, it is so important for the salesperson (product specialist or wholesaler) to develop her own relationship with the end prospect (a task that can be difficult because, as we mentioned earlier, the intermediary may want to control the process). This is similar to what we described when you enter into a company at the wrong level with a key influencer prospect who is not the true decision maker; you sometimes get boxed into a certain level and flow of information. Your intermediary may not want you to have a relationship with the end prospect because he may be insecure about his position in the sales process or may feel that you may do or say something that will negatively reflect on the intermediary.

Due to all of these factors, selling through intermediaries can often cause a serious overlap of issues that can conspire to work

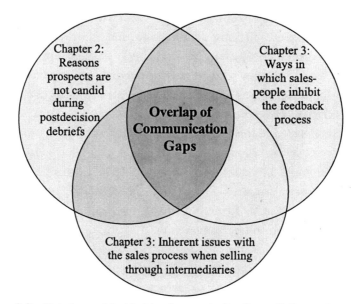

Figure 3.3 Main Areas of Postdecision Communication Gaps with Prospects

against you in getting the truth about why you win and lose. For a visual representation of this situation, see Figure 3.3.

Figure 3.3 highlights the challenges salespeople face when selling through intermediaries in order to give you a clearer picture of all the communication gap overlap areas.

If your sales process involves selling through intermediaries, the process of getting candid and honest feedback from prospects post-decision can be even more challenging than normal. Not only will many of your prospects be unwilling to be forthcoming and candid, but you as a salesperson may be hindering yourself from getting candid feedback. Lastly, the intermediary may block you from ever speaking with the prospect, and,

> If your sales process involves selling through intermediaries, the process of getting candid and honest feedback from prospects postdecision can be even more challenging than normal.

as a result, you may never really fully understand why you win and lose in new business situations. As Figure 3.3 shows, all of these silos may overlap and work together to conspire against your ever learning what you do well and not so well.

CHAPTER WRAP-UP

Although all of the areas we explored in this chapter illustrate ways in which salespeople inhibit the feedback process, this chapter is not intended to criticize salespeople; rather, it is intended to enhance your abilities and success. There is no doubt that the sales profession is challenging, but perhaps the biggest challenge for a salesperson is acquiring full insights and understanding into why she wins and loses in new business situations. Without these insights, it can be difficult to accurately assess areas for improvement.

All of the issues mentioned in this chapter prevent salespeople from fully understanding their prospects—a dangerous proposition, since prospects determine where a company is going. The good news is that this situation can be alleviated by better incorporating a critical element into your sales process: a formal postdecision debrief. Debriefing with prospects after a sales decision has been made is the critical final element to the sales process. In fact, *93 percent of salespeople feel that postdecision debriefs are a valuable exercise that can help them win more business in the future.*

As we've shown in the last two chapters, there are many reasons salespeople have difficulty getting accurate feedback from prospects postdecision. Now that you understand the problem, you are well positioned to counteract these obstacles. Remember, it is only after you fully understand a problem that you can begin to work on a solution.

In Part 1 of this book, I have shown you not only what can be gained by learning how to effectively debrief with prospects but also the full range of challenges that salespeople face when they attempt to interview prospects postdecision. This information provides an important foundation for your learning as we move into Part 2, where you will learn easy-to-implement tips and techniques on how to properly conduct debriefs with prospects. Part 2 will give you the working tools you need to reap the benefits discussed in Chapter 1 while avoiding the pitfalls we explored in Chapters 2 and 3.

CHAPTER SUMMARY

Ways in Which Sales Reps Inhibit the Feedback Process

- Sales reps are not in an objective position to obtain feedback.
- Sales reps may be caught off guard by a bad news call and may be unprepared for conducting a debrief.
- Sales reps usually do not know the right questions to ask (and how to ask them) because most sales professionals have historically overlooked and poorly utilized prospect debriefs.
  - Historically there has been very little study and literature on postdecision debriefs.
  - Sales training and sales seminars rarely cover how to appropriately conduct postdecision debriefs and what the benefits are of the process.
  - Most sales managers do not have formal win/loss analysis programs in place that gauge why they win and lose business.
- Sales reps typically do not debrief with bids won prospects to better understand why they won (and what they can do better).
- It can be very difficult to ascertain the true reasons for loss if you are not selling directly to the decision maker.
- When salespeople sell through intermediaries, channels, or partners, it can often be difficult to have direct contact with the end prospect and therefore gather any meaningful postdecision feedback from prospects.

Sales Statistics

- The average salesperson conducts win reviews with new customers only 40 percent of the time and loss reviews 45 percent of the time.
- According to 93 percent of salespeople, postdecision debriefs are a valuable exercise that can help them win more business in the future.

· · · · · · · · · · · · ·

PART 2

SELF-DIAGNOSING YOUR SALES EFFECTIVENESS THROUGH POSTDECISION DEBRIEFS WITH PROSPECTS

· · · · · · · · · · · · · · ·

Design a Prospect Debrief Questionnaire

Now that you understand the many benefits that can be gained by conducting more in-depth debriefs and you have learned why debriefing with prospects is such a challenging part of the sales process, the next step is to learn how to improve your postdecision conversations with prospects.

The first step in learning how to conduct better postdecision debriefs is to identify the full range of sales process and product/service areas that you will review with each prospect. The best way to do this is by designing a comprehensive debrief questionnaire. You will find that by investing upfront energy into drafting a questionnaire, you will reap the many benefits of the information that this conversation guide will provide to you.

This chapter has three sections. First, we will review the benefits of using a formal questionnaire. Next, we will examine the various question types that need to be included in the questionnaire design. Lastly, we will show you two sample questionnaires (one for bids lost situations and one for bids won situations) that you can use as prototypes for designing your own debrief guide.

USE A DEBRIEF QUESTIONNAIRE

The best thing you can do to ensure that you get the most comprehensive feedback from prospects is to draft a customized interview questionnaire. This simple process will ensure that you are consistently getting the most out of your postdecision discussions. Currently, only 25 percent of salespeople use a formal written questionnaire when conducting postdecision debriefs. This means 75 percent of salespeople are entering into these conversations unprepared and debriefing with prospects in a disorganized way.

> Only 25 percent of salespeople use a formal written questionnaire when conducting postdecision debriefs.

By not using a questionnaire, salespeople continue to lose a great opportunity to obtain more consistent, candid feedback and information from prospects. If you are going to conduct the debrief anyway, it only makes sense to take the next step and plan out your line of questioning in a written format. You will find that it organizes your thinking, makes the whole process smoother, and allows you to gather more actionable information.

Here are four key reasons it is important to use a written questionnaire when conducting postdecision debriefs.

Increase Your Close Rate by 15 Percent

The most compelling reason to develop and use a debrief questionnaire is that salespeople who use their own debrief questionnaires have a 15 percent higher close rate than salespeople who do not. Period.

This data clearly indicates that salespeople who take the time to get organized in their questioning win more business. Salespeople who use a questionnaire simply gather more detailed feedback on themselves, the competition, and their companies' products and services when debriefing with prospects, and this ultimately allows them to apply what they learn back into subsequent sales cycles. If this

> Salespeople who use their own debrief questionnaires have a 15 percent higher close rate than salespeople who do not.

statistic doesn't convince you to draft and use your own survey guide, I don't know what will.

Maximize Feedback and Keep the Conversation Focused

Using a formal survey will help you get better information because the prospect will take the conversation more seriously and will work harder to give you better and more meaningful feedback. People tend to put more effort into a discussion when they know you have a specific list of questions and are taking notes.

Using a survey template will help to keep the prospect focused on the key topics of the deal. It will also help you, as the interviewer, stay on point and not wander off onto various elements of the discussion that may be less fruitful.

Additionally, using a questionnaire ensures that you always ask the right questions. Have you ever gotten off the phone after debriefing with a prospect and said to yourself, "I should have asked the prospect that question"? Salespeople often come to this realization when discussing why they lost with their sales managers or senior management at their companies. If you are like most salespeople, you often forget to ask prospects certain questions. This is problematic, because you usually have only one shot to make this kind of call with the prospect. It can be awkward to go back to a prospect with additional questions after you have completed a debrief. Therefore, by thinking through your questions in advance, you will be in a much better position to ensure that you ask all the right questions, all the time. Without a written guide, it is highly likely that key questions will be forgotten or left out during feedback sessions.

If you're still questioning the value of a formal questionnaire, consider this: Let's suppose that my firm, which conducts win/loss analysis for Fortune 500 companies, entered into an engagement with your sales team to perform independent win/loss interviews. What do you think would happen if I told your head of sales that we were not going to use a questionnaire and that we were just going to "wing it" when we spoke with prospects over the phone? Do you think your head of sales would allow this? The truth is that you would not allow a market research firm to speak to your prospects or clients without a scripted questionnaire, yet salespeople do this in their interactions with prospects all the time.

Take Organized Notes

Using a questionnaire also allows you to take notes in an organized manner. This is one reason that when the head of a sales team hires an outside firm to conduct win/loss analysis work, the first thing the outside firm does is to design a questionnaire. This allows all parties involved to make sure they are asking all the right questions, and it also allows the interviewer to take organized notes as the interview is conducted. This is unquestionably the most productive way to conduct a postdecision interview.

If you take notes on your questionnaire, this will leave you with an incredible resource you can use if you ever engage with the same prospect or company again. By writing down the prospect's responses, you will have a "road map" of what went well and not so well during the sales process. It may be years before you interact with the prospect again, so you will find it quite helpful to be able to return to the document after time has passed and recall the specifics of why you lost the deal the first time.

Important: take notes by hand. Do not type or use a computer while you are speaking with a prospect during a debrief. It is okay to take notes by hand because this is a relatively silent process, but typing is distracting to prospects when you are speaking with them. It will also distract you and negatively impact your ability to make the interview conversational. Additionally, you should not do anything else while speaking with a prospect, such as checking your e-mail or shuffling papers in the background. Even if you think you are being quiet, the person on the other end of the phone can tell when you are distracted, and this can limit your discussion.

> Take notes by hand. Do not type or use a computer while you are speaking with a prospect during a debrief.

Once Developed, Your Questionnaire Can Be Used for the Rest of Your Career

Once developed, a formal questionnaire is an invaluable tool you can utilize and refine throughout your career (no matter what company you sell for). Once you develop a written guide you feel comfortable with, you can take it with you anywhere in your career. If you move to a sales job in the same industry with a similar product or service, you can very easily use the same questionnaire; just customize it to your new company's products or services. Even if you move to a sales job in a different industry, you can still modify this existing document quite easily.

This process can also be valuable to sales professionals who are new to selling. In fact, a win/loss program can help new sales reps leapfrog ahead of where they would normally be if they were to just continue learning their lessons the hard way. Using a postdecision debrief questionnaire can help you to learn about your sales performance, industry, competitive landscape, and products and services much quicker, and, as a result, you will improve your sales performance at a faster rate.

Now that we have explored why using a formal questionnaire is so important, let's look at a few key question types that should be considered when designing a debrief questionnaire.

KEY QUESTION TYPES

There are four critical components that should be included in your questionnaire: evaluation of decision-making criteria, qualitative strength and weakness questioning, benchmarking/questions about the competition, and specific questions pertaining to areas of the sales process that could have been done differently to better position yourself, your company, and/or your product and service offering. A review of each of these types of questions will help you better understand how to craft a postdecision debrief questionnaire that best suits your industry as well as your own unique needs.

Let's review each type of question so that you can become familiar with how and why each questioning strategy is useful to you.

Evaluation of Decision-Making Criteria Questions

Questions that evaluate a prospect's principal decision-making criteria can help you determine whether or not you were able to assess

* In the end, what were the four most important decision-making criteria you used when differentiating between competitors?
* For each of these criteria, how did my firm compare to the firm you chose?

Criteria:	Much better	Slightly better	Equal	Slightly worse	Much worse
Attribute 1	☐	☐	☐	☐	☐
Attribute 2	☐	☐	☐	☐	☐
Attribute 3	☐	☐	☐	☐	☐
Attribute 4	☐	☐	☐	☐	☐

(Note to sales rep: If prospect rates you "worse than" the competition, probe to find out why.)

Figure 4.1 Sample Questionnaire Format for Probing a Prospect's Decision-Making Criteria

accurately what the prospect was looking for during the sales process. As Chapter 7 will show, one of the main reasons salespeople lose deals is they do not accurately understand the unique needs of their prospects. By approaching prospects after the fact to review their exact needs and ascertain whether or not you adequately addressed them, you will learn how to better assess these areas in the future.

Figure 4.1 shows two examples of prospect decision-making criteria questions. These questions work well at the beginning of the discussion because they get the prospect talking and are not too obtrusive. They also get the prospect back into the frame of mind of the sales process, allowing her to recall what she was looking for when contemplating her decision. These questions are also important in helping to break the prospect's concentration from whatever she was working on prior to your call.

Qualitative Strength and Weakness Questions

Qualitative strength and weakness questions are open-ended questions designed to let the prospect think and answer free form. Open-ended questions such as these do not box the prospect into any specific type of answer and instead are designed to get the prospect talking and opening up to provide candid feedback. Qualitative questions are very useful when assessing sales process issues because the sales process has always been and will always be more of an art than a science. If you have ever sold a product or service, you know it is very difficult to quantify anything in the sales process because so much of the sale has to do with how well you read the prospect and address what he is looking for.

Here are some examples of qualitative strength and weakness questions:

* What are our strong points?
* Where could we improve?
* When you look back on our company's products and services, what are our strong points?
* When you look back on our company's products and services, what could we improve?
* When you look back on the sales process and sales presentation, what were my/our strong points?
* When you look back on the sales process and sales presentation, where could I/we improve?
* Compared with the other firms' presentations/presentation teams, what did I/our team do well? Not as well?

These strengths and weaknesses questions allow the prospect to brainstorm and think about what you did well and not so well during the sales process. These questions are the most important ones in your survey because they get at what you really want to know from the prospect. Due to the importance of these questions, I recommend not starting right away with them. Instead, look to ask these questions about 25 percent of the way into each interview.

The reason for this is twofold. One, you do not want to ask these questions at the beginning of the survey because the prospect might feel it is too early to answer such tough questions. In a sense, you need to warm up the prospect and get her talking so she will be in a groove to give you this critical feedback. Just as you strive to get the prospect talking at the beginning of the sales process, you want to get her talking at the beginning of the debrief.

The second reason you should ask these questions later in the survey is that prospects are often distracted with all the other things they need to do during a typical workday. Therefore, you need to make sure you have the prospect's full attention before asking the most important questions. In fact, it generally takes about three to five minutes before a prospect is fully engaged in a debrief conversation. My company has found that it takes about that long for the respondent to disengage from his last meeting or the topic of discussion in which he was involved before he got on the phone with you. As humans, we tend to need time to switch gears, so to speak, so don't ask these questions too early because you will not get the best and most accurate answers.

> It generally takes about three to five minutes before a prospect is fully engaged in a debrief conversation.

This is yet another reason it is so important to set up a separate and distinct call when you debrief with prospects postdecision. As we explored in Chapter 2, when prospects initially give you the bad news about losing the deal, their mind-set is one in which they want to get you off the phone as quickly as possible; therefore, they may only want to spend three to five minutes with you for the entire conversation. This often leaves them unable to shift gears and gather momentum to actually get into a constructive conversation. Ultimately, if you don't set up a separate call, you will find that prospects are never able to fully engage in your conversation and give you accurate feedback.

I highly recommend asking strengths and weaknesses questions after you've already warmed up the prospect.

Benchmarking Questions/Assessment of the Competition

Benchmarking questions are most valuable when you want to compare yourself or your firm to the competition. They give the prospect a clear way to grade you versus other players in your marketplace and rate you in a comprehensive way.

See Figure 4.2 for some examples of benchmarking questions.

In this section, I will read a list of attributes and I'd like you to rate my performance and my company's performance relative to the winning firm.

Name of Winning Firm:

Criteria:	Much better than winning firm	Slightly better than winning firm	Equal to winning firm	Slightly worse than winning firm	Much worse than winning firm
Sales Process/Presentation					
Proposal/RFP response	☐	☐	☐	☐	☐
My presentation/our presentation	☐	☐	☐	☐	☐
Customization of the presentation	☐	☐	☐	☐	☐

(Note to sales rep: If prospect rated you "worse than" the winning firm on any attribute(s), probe to find out why.)

Figure 4.2   Sample Benchmarking Questions

For the purposes of your debrief, in bids lost situations, your competition would be whoever won the deal; for bids won situations, your competition would be the second-place (runner-up) firm.

Questions pertaining to the competition are critical because any insights you gain about your competition will allow you to better differentiate yourself and your firm in the future. These questions help you understand to whom you lost the business and why. These questions also allow you to determine if your company has any product or service gaps.

Here are three additional examples of questions designed to get the prospect talking about the competition:

* What were your top reasons for choosing the winning firm?
* Did the other competitors present anything that is not currently offered by our company?
* With respect to the firm you chose, what is the one thing that if they didn't have, would have made you choose us?

These questions are best asked toward the end of the survey because the prospect will already be engaged and talking freely. The prospect will also sense that you are nearing the end of the discussion and therefore may give in to providing you truly valuable competitive intelligence.

Specific Targeted Questions about the Deal

While the three previous question types can be used in all of your debriefs, specific targeted questions focus on particular areas where you feel you could have performed better on each specific deal. For example, you may have said something or had a situation during a sales process that you think might not have gone over well with the prospect. Or you may have a hunch regarding why you lost a specific deal that you want to examine. You should ask these types of questions at the very end of the survey so that even if the prospect feels awkward answering the question, you will be done with the debrief shortly thereafter.

Deal-specific questions will likely vary for each particular sales situation, so you will need to draft these questions in advance of each of your debrief calls. Do not worry too much about how to ask these questions; just ask them in the most genuine way possible (and ask them at the end of the survey).

Now that we have explored all the different types of questions in a postdecision interview, let's look at a couple of sample questionnaires you can use as starting points for building your own questionnaire.

SAMPLE WIN/LOSS QUESTIONNAIRES

This section provides two sample questionnaires, including helpful tips and explanations on how to best use the surveys. The first questionnaire is for lost deal situations, and the second is for situations in which you won the business. You will see that these questionnaires are very similar, with only a few wording changes depending on whether the deal was won or lost.

Please note that you can receive a complimentary download of these documents from our Web site at www.theanovagroup.com/debriefguide.htm (password: winloss). These documents will come to you in a Word document format so you can begin using them right away.

Sample Postdecision Debrief Guide:
Deals Lost

Prospect Name:_____

Prospect Company:_____

"Mr. Prospect, thank you very much for speaking with me today. I really appreciate it. These feedback calls help us to ensure that we are working on the right issues instead of having to guess what needs improvement during our sales process and to our products and services.

"I want to let you know up front that your feedback isn't going to get anyone in trouble. Our company is committed to improving on everything we do, and we view these calls as a critical opportunity to help us achieve that end goal.

"So please be as candid as possible. I am totally open to any constructive feedback you may have (including feedback directly related to my personal performance) because it will ultimately help me do my job better and be more successful."

Here's an example of how to introduce the call. Chapter 5 will outline in-depth techniques on how to get the interview started in the most effective way.

Decision-Making Criteria Questions

1. In the end, what were the three most important decision-making criteria you used when differentiating between competitors?

_____

_____

_____

2. For each of the above-mentioned criteria, how did my firm compare with the firm you chose?

Criteria	Much better	Slightly better	Equal	Slightly worse	Much worse
1.	☐	☐	☐	☐	☐
2.	☐	☐	☐	☐	☐
3.	☐	☐	☐	☐	☐

If rating is worse than the competition, probe to find out why.

_____

_____

_____

3. How was the decision made? Who were the key decision makers during the sales process?

_____

_____

_____

Qualitative Strengths and Weaknesses Questions ——————

> Strengths and weaknesses are split into two subcategories: *Products and Services* and *Sales Process/ Presentation.*

4. When you look back on our company's <u>products and services</u>, what are our strong points?

_____

_____

_____

5. When you look back on our company's <u>products and services</u>, what could we improve?

_____

_____

_____

6. When you look back on the <u>sales process, proposal, and sales presentation</u>, what were my/our strong points?

_____

_____

_____

7. When you look back on the <u>sales process, proposal, and sales presentation</u>, where could I/we improve?

_____

_____

_____

8. Compared with the other firms' presentations/presentation teams, what did I/ our team do well? Not as well?

_____

_____

_____

Benchmarking Questions/Assessment of the Competition

For the next group of questions, I'd like you to rate my performance and my company's performance relative to the winning firm.

Name of Winning Firm:

<table>
<tr><th>Criteria</th><th>Much better than winning firm</th><th>Slightly better than winning firm</th><th>Equal to winning firm</th><th>Slightly worse than winning firm</th><th>Much worse than winning firm</th></tr>
<tr><td>**Sales Process/Presentation**</td><td></td><td></td><td></td><td></td><td></td></tr>
<tr><td>Proposal/RFP response</td><td>☐</td><td>☐</td><td>☐</td><td>☐</td><td>☐</td></tr>
<tr><td>My presentation/our presentation</td><td>☐</td><td>☐</td><td>☐</td><td>☐</td><td>☐</td></tr>
<tr><td>Customization of presentation</td><td>☐</td><td>☐</td><td>☐</td><td>☐</td><td>☐</td></tr>
<tr><td>Presentation materials/brochures</td><td>☐</td><td>☐</td><td>☐</td><td>☐</td><td>☐</td></tr>
<tr><td>(If applicable) Our corporate Web site</td><td>☐</td><td>☐</td><td>☐</td><td>☐</td><td>☐</td></tr>
<tr><td>(If applicable) References</td><td>☐</td><td>☐</td><td>☐</td><td>☐</td><td>☐</td></tr>
<tr><td>(If applicable) Site visit</td><td>☐</td><td>☐</td><td>☐</td><td>☐</td><td>☐</td></tr>
<tr><td>**Salesperson**</td><td></td><td></td><td></td><td></td><td></td></tr>
<tr><td>My overall preparedness</td><td>☐</td><td>☐</td><td>☐</td><td>☐</td><td>☐</td></tr>
<tr><td>My ability to make you feel you would be valued as a customer</td><td>☐</td><td>☐</td><td>☐</td><td>☐</td><td>☐</td></tr>
<tr><td>My ability to understand your unique needs and provide solutions</td><td>☐</td><td>☐</td><td>☐</td><td>☐</td><td>☐</td></tr>
<tr><td>My responsiveness</td><td>☐</td><td>☐</td><td>☐</td><td>☐</td><td>☐</td></tr>
<tr><td>My product/industry knowledge</td><td>☐</td><td>☐</td><td>☐</td><td>☐</td><td>☐</td></tr>
<tr><td colspan="6">**Sales Team/Presentation** (If other people present with you at the sales meeting/presentation)</td></tr>
<tr><td>Other presentation team participant #1</td><td>☐</td><td>☐</td><td>☐</td><td>☐</td><td>☐</td></tr>
<tr><td>Other presentation team participant #2</td><td>☐</td><td>☐</td><td>☐</td><td>☐</td><td>☐</td></tr>
<tr><td>Cohesiveness of our sales team</td><td>☐</td><td>☐</td><td>☐</td><td>☐</td><td>☐</td></tr>
<tr><td>**Products and Services**</td><td></td><td></td><td></td><td></td><td></td></tr>
<tr><td>Client service quality</td><td>☐</td><td>☐</td><td>☐</td><td>☐</td><td>☐</td></tr>
<tr><td>Pricing</td><td>☐</td><td>☐</td><td>☐</td><td>☐</td><td>☐</td></tr>
<tr><td>Technological capabilities</td><td>☐</td><td>☐</td><td>☐</td><td>☐</td><td>☐</td></tr>
<tr><td>Brand/reputation</td><td>☐</td><td>☐</td><td>☐</td><td>☐</td><td>☐</td></tr>
<tr><td>Specific product/service feature #1</td><td>☐</td><td>☐</td><td>☐</td><td>☐</td><td>☐</td></tr>
<tr><td>Specific product/service feature #2</td><td>☐</td><td>☐</td><td>☐</td><td>☐</td><td>☐</td></tr>
<tr><td>Specific product/service feature #3</td><td>☐</td><td>☐</td><td>☐</td><td>☐</td><td>☐</td></tr>
</table>

(Note to sales rep: If prospect rated you "worse than" the winning firm on any attribute(s), probe to find out why.)

_____

_____

_____

Adjust wording of question depending on whether you were the sole presenter or there were other people presenting with you (i.e., team selling).

If you sense the prospect feels uncomfortable discussing actual fee numbers, consider asking about a percentage differential. Also, if the prospect rates you "worse than" the winning firm, probe to determine whether it was actual price or an issue with clarity of pricing.

Ask prospect to rate specific product or service features. For example, if you're selling enterprise software, perhaps you're interested in their perception of the reporting capabilities or ease of use.

9. What were the top reasons for choosing the winning firm?

_____

_____

_____

10. Did the other competitors present anything that is not currently offered by our company?

_____

_____

_____

11. When do you think you will review this decision/your product and service needs again?

_____

_____

_____

12. Have I missed anything? What else should I be asking?

_____

_____

_____

Prospect Specific/Deal Specific Questions

Question 1?

_____

_____

_____

Question 2?

_____

_____

_____

Use the end of the debrief to probe any specific areas where you feel you could have performed better. For example, if you think you lost the deal because you didn't bring a technical person to the meeting, probe to find out if this influenced the decision and ask whether the competition did so

Sample Postdecision Debrief Guide:
Deals Won

Prospect Name:_____

Prospect Company:_____

"Mr. Prospect, thank you very much for speaking with me today, and thank you for your business. I really appreciate it. These feedback calls help us to ensure that we are working on the right issues instead of having to guess what needs improvement during our sales process and to our products and services.

"I want to let you know up front that your feedback isn't going to get anyone in trouble. Our company is committed to improving on everything we do, and we view these calls as a critical opportunity to help us achieve that end goal.

"So please be as candid as possible. I am totally open to any constructive feedback you may have (including feedback directly related to my personal performance) because it will ultimately help me do my job better and be more successful."

Decision-Making Criteria Questions

1. In the end, what were the three most important decision-making criteria you used when differentiating between competitors?

_____

_____

_____

2. For each of the above-mentioned criteria, how did my firm compare to the competition:

Criteria	Much better	Slightly better	Equal	Slightly worse	Much worse
1.	☐	☐	☐	☐	☐
2.	☐	☐	☐	☐	☐
3.	☐	☐	☐	☐	☐

(Note to sales rep: If prospect rated you "worse than" the competition, probe to find out why.)

_____

_____

_____

3. How was the decision made? Who were the key decision makers during the sales process?

_____

_____

_____

Qualitative Strengths and Weaknesses Questions

4. When you look back on our company's <u>products and services</u>, what are our strong points?

_____

_____

_____

5. When you look back on our company's <u>products and services</u>, what could we improve?

_____

_____

_____

6. When you look back on the <u>sales process, proposal, and sales presentation</u>, what were my/our strong points?

_____

_____

_____

7. When you look back on the <u>sales process, proposal, and sales presentation</u>, where could I/we improve?

_____

_____

_____

8. Compared with the other firms' presentations/presentation teams, what did I/our team do well? Not as well?

_____

_____

_____

Benchmarking Questions/Assessment of the Competition

In this section, I will read a list of attributes and I'd like you to rate my performance and my company's performance relative to the second-place firm.

Name of 2nd-Place Firm:

Criteria	Much better than 2nd-place firm	Slightly better than 2nd-place firm	Equal to 2nd-place firm	Slightly worse than 2nd-place firm	Much worse than 2nd-place firm
Sales Process/Presentation					
Proposal/RFP response	☐	☐	☐	☐	☐
My presentation/our presentation	☐	☐	☐	☐	☐
Customization of presentation	☐	☐	☐	☐	☐
Presentation materials/brochures	☐	☐	☐	☐	☐
(If applicable) Our corporate Web site	☐	☐	☐	☐	☐
(If applicable) References	☐	☐	☐	☐	☐
(If applicable) Site visit	☐	☐	☐	☐	☐
Salesperson					
My overall preparedness	☐	☐	☐	☐	☐
My ability to make you feel you would be valued as a customer	☐	☐	☐	☐	☐
My ability to understand your unique needs and provide solutions	☐	☐	☐	☐	☐
My responsiveness	☐	☐	☐	☐	☐
My product/industry knowledge	☐	☐	☐	☐	☐
Sales Team/Presentation *(If other people present with you at the sales meeting/presentation)*					
Other presentation team participant #1	☐	☐	☐	☐	☐
Other presentation team participant #2	☐	☐	☐	☐	☐
Cohesiveness of our sales team	☐	☐	☐	☐	☐
Products and Services					
Client service quality	☐	☐	☐	☐	☐
Pricing	☐	☐	☐	☐	☐
Technological capabilities	☐	☐	☐	☐	☐
Brand/reputation	☐	☐	☐	☐	☐
Specific product/service feature #1	☐	☐	☐	☐	☐
Specific product/service feature #2	☐	☐	☐	☐	☐
Specific product/service feature #3	☐	☐	☐	☐	☐

(Note to sales rep: If prospect rated you "worse than" the competition on any attribute(s), probe to find out why.)

_____

_____

_____

9. What other companies did you speak with during the sales process?

_____

_____

_____

10. Did the other competitors present anything that is not currently offered by our company?

_____

_____

_____

11. When do you think you will receive this decision/your product and service needs again?

_____

_____

_____

12. Have I missed anything? What else should I be asking?

_____

_____

_____

Prospect Specific/Deal Specific Questions

Question 1?

_____

_____

_____

Question 2?

_____

_____

_____

These questionnaires provide you with a starting point for a comprehensive and effective prospect debrief, and you can customize them to your company's products, services, and sales process.

You do not need to use all these questions; you can customize your survey template any way you like. Although results vary from prospect to prospect, we have found that an average interview can last anywhere from 10 to 15 minutes (though some can go considerably longer if the prospect is engaged, anywhere up to 40 minutes); therefore, don't make the mistake of making your questionnaire too short.

CHAPTER WRAP-UP

There is an ancient Chinese proverb that says, "He who asks is a fool for five minutes, but he who does not ask remains a fool forever." Having an organized questionnaire and asking great questions at the end of each sales cycle is a great way to learn from your successes and failures. Remember, salespeople who use a questionnaire when debriefing with prospects have a 15 percent higher close rate than salespeople who do not.

There are many benefits to using a formal document as a guide to conducting your postdecision debriefs with prospects. When you use a questionnaire to conduct win/loss debriefs, you will be more prepared and look more professional. Using a questionnaire allows you to end your sales cycle on a positive note and will leave all of your won and lost prospects silently impressed. Ask yourself, who will look better in the prospect's eyes, the salesperson who conducts an unplanned feedback call, or the salesperson who takes the time to prepare and uses a questionnaire? Also, who do you think will be more likely to get future business from the prospect?

Now that you understand the different question types and questioning strategies and have customized your own debrief guide, you are almost ready to get on the phone with your lost and won prospects. In the next chapter, I will show you strategies for how to best set up your postdecision interviews with prospects, and I will also show you proven interviewing techniques that will help you get the most out of your questionnaire and take your debrief conversations to the next level.

CHAPTER SUMMARY

The Benefits of Using a Postdecision Debrief Questionnaire

* Salespeople who use a debrief questionnaire have a 15 percent higher close rate.
* Using a questionnaire maximizes feedback and keeps the conversation focused.
* A questionnaire allows you to easily take organized notes. This can be a valuable source of information that can be referred back to in the future should you reengage with the prospect.
* Once developed, a formal questionnaire is an invaluable tool you can utilize and refine throughout your career (no matter what company you sell for).

Key Question Types for Postdecision Debrief Questionnaires

* *Evaluation of key decision-making criteria.* Questions to help you better understand what the prospect's unique needs were and how he made his decision.
* *Qualitative strength and weakness questions.* Open-ended questions designed to get the prospect talking about you and your company's strengths and weaknesses.
* *Benchmarking/assessment of the competition.* Questions designed to allow the prospect to easily rate you and benchmark you against your competition. Questions for competitive intelligence.
* *Specific prospect/deal questions.* Questions that address areas of the sales process that can be difficult to discuss. These questions should be asked at the end of the debrief.

Sample Postdecision Debrief Questionnaires (Lost and Won Deals)

* Can be downloaded at www.theanovagroup.com/debriefguide.htm (password: winloss).
* Can be customized in Word to your unique sales process and your company's products and services.

Utilize Proven Interviewing Techniques for Conducting Debrief Calls

Now that you have designed your own comprehensive prospect debrief questionnaire, it is time to learn the skills you will need to conduct the interviews successfully. Having a questionnaire brings you a long way toward a successful interview; however, it is equally important to know how to set up a call and how to conduct yourself during the debrief. In this chapter, you will learn tested techniques for initiating and conducting thorough postloss debriefs.

This chapter is divided into three sections:

1. How to set up the debrief call.
2. How to act during a postdecision debrief call.
3. How to probe and gather the most valuable information using proven interview techniques.

Let's begin by looking at the best way to set up a debrief call.

HOW TO SET UP A POSTDECISION DEBRIEF CALL

One of the most critical parts of the whole feedback process is to make sure you know how to correctly ask the prospect for a postdecision debrief. You must start the process off on the right foot; otherwise, the prospect will not be as forthcoming with information (as we've explored in Chapter 2). When selling, everything you say and do counts. Everything either works for or against you, and this is no different at the end of the process when you are setting up and conducting debrief calls. It is critical to make sure everything you do and say when setting up the call lets the prospect know that you are professional and that you are looking for candid feedback and guidance.

Get Approval for the Debrief Early in the Sales Process

The first step is to let your prospects know early in the sales process that you will be conducting a debrief with them no matter how the sales process plays out. This is something few salespeople do. As we saw in Chapter 3, many salespeople do not even conduct post-decision debriefs, and those who do usually do not perform them correctly. Salespeople typically wait until the end of the process to request a debrief, a less than optimal approach. It is better to let the prospect know early on in the sales process so you plant a seed in the prospect's mind. By taking this proactive step, you are setting a foundation for the debrief call that will create an implied agreement with the prospect for an interview.

Asking for the postdecision debrief early in the sales process also builds credibility for you and your company. This "win or lose, I'd like your perspective" approach reinforces the concept of a consultative sales process while also providing reciprocity for the efforts you as the sales professional are about to invest. In fact, the very act of asking for this information creates a kind of counterbalance within the sales process. By taking this approach, you are letting the prospect know you are going to put in a lot of time and effort during the sales process and would like feedback in return.

Remember, you and your company spend significant time and money selling to buyers. In fact, it has been estimated that a typical sales process can cost a company 5 percent of the total average annual revenue of a client or buyer. For example, if you are selling a product or service that will bring in annual revenue of $1 million to your company, it is likely that your organization will spend approximately $50,000 in sales costs. These costs include expenses such as your salary and commission, travel costs, team selling expenses, costs

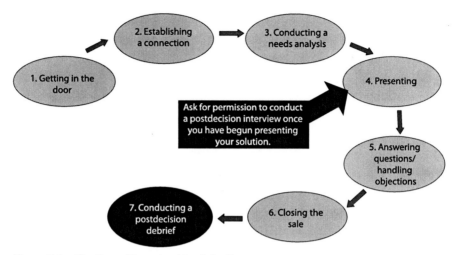

Figure 5.1   The Seven Elements of the Sales Process

related to preparing an RFP, printing costs for sales materials, and so on. These costs occur whether you win or lose the deal, so don't be afraid to let prospects know early in the sales process that you and your company conduct in-depth postdecision debriefs at the end of every sales cycle, and that you do this because you and your company have a culture of continuous improvement.

When is the best time during the sales process to notify the prospect that you will be conducting a postdecision debrief? As Figure 5.1 shows, the best time to ask is after you have built rapport with the buyer and identified his needs. Then, when you are beginning your process of presenting solutions, you can mention it to the prospect. Additionally, if possible, ask this question when you are face to face with the prospect. Let the prospect know it is part of the sales process at your company, and ask him if it would be okay for you to interview him postdecision.

Here's an example of how to ask for a postdecision debrief during the sales process (feel free to fine-tune this into whatever conversational approach you feel best suits your style):

Mr. Prospect, I wanted to let you know that after the whole sales process is done, I would like to conduct a debrief call with you. I would like to debrief with you no matter what decision you finally make. This is part of our company's process because we are always striving for improvement in both our sales process and with our products and services. Would it be okay for us to debrief after you've made your final decision?

This is yet another great sales question you can add to your arsenal of question-based selling techniques. In fact, prospects love this question; it implies that you are professional and that your company has high standards. This question should take you no more than one minute to execute. Very rarely will a prospect say "no" to this request if asked early on during the sales process because you are asking for something that is a professional courtesy, and the call is not going to happen right away; therefore, it does not immediately impact the prospect. Also, at this point, the prospect is engaged, and she understands you are putting in time and effort on the sales process. Remember, there is a certain amount of reciprocity and obligation that can be used in getting debrief information.

You should also let any intermediaries that are involved know that postdecision debriefs are a part of your process. As we reviewed in Chapter 3, an intermediary is anyone outside your firm who is involved in the sales process and works between you and the buyer (such as a consultant who has been hired by the prospect to help make a buying decision). If you sell with or through any type of intermediary channel regularly, you need to notify them only once about your process of conducting postdecision interviews.

Many of my clients have used the process of early prospect notification successfully to ensure that the prospect knows that the company takes the sales process very seriously. This process is critical for setting the stage for an optimal postdecision debrief.

Do Not Debrief When You First Learn You Have Lost the Deal

The most common mistake salespeople make when they debrief with lost prospects is attempting to gather feedback during the same call in which they learn they have lost the deal. As we explored in Chapters 2 and 3, this is a major mistake and, in most cases, you will not get any meaningful feedback from prospects during this discussion.

Additionally, emotions run extremely high during these tense situations (for both the prospect and the salesperson), and this is why time needs to pass before you can begin thinking straight again. In fact, emotions such as these cause most businesspeople to shy away from careers

> **The most common mistake salespeople make when they debrief with lost prospects is attempting to gather feedback during the same call in which they learn they have lost the deal.**

in sales in the first place. No one enjoys going through rejection, and it takes a lot of self-confidence and emotional intelligence to withstand this type of situation regularly. Whatever emotions you have at this point will inhibit your ability to successfully debrief with a prospect. You need time to reflect and regain composure after defeat. It is virtually impossible for you to have all the right questions to ask at this particular moment and to ask them in the right frame of mind.

Try to remember it's not personal. You are just doing your job, and emotions like anger, regret, fear, and sadness do you no good. This situation has as much to do with psychology as it does with the sales process. Anytime anything comes to an end, emotions are heightened. When something ends, be it a relationship, job, school year, sales process, or anything else, humans become emotional, and therefore it is often difficult to gain a full perspective during these times.

Can you see how this situation is not conducive to a successful debrief? Yet this is what most salespeople do. They go right into a debrief line of questioning and are typically met with a prospect who does not want to have a detailed discussion. This is one of the main reasons that most of what we explored in Chapters 2 and 3 occurs. In fact, most salespeople think they are debriefing prospects properly, but they are not; they are trying to extract feedback information at the worst point in the sales cycle. Don't let this happen to you.

As an example that demonstrates this less than optimal approach, one recurring theme I have witnessed over many years of working with companies is that typically a CRM database will be used to track the reasons for sales losses. When you analyze the reasons for losing that are entered into the database by the sales team, you will often find that there is only one word or one reason entered. You might see something like "price" or a certain missing product feature listed as the reason for loss. However, the reasons for losing are always more complex than one-word answers. Most salespeople conduct debriefs right when the prospects call to tell them they lost; salespeople tend to get very short and brief reasons for loss or even inaccurate and incomplete reasons.

I am not saying you should not have a short conversation about the reasons for losing. It is perfectly fine to ask, "What happened?" and allow the prospect to talk. In fact, it would be odd if you don't have a conversation about this topic. However, don't expect to get a lot of information; just accept the loss gracefully and professionally. Tell the prospect you are disappointed but that you understand and wish her the best of luck in the future. Once you have done this, then is the time to set up the postloss debrief call.

This is all part of keeping the correct flow of the sales process. Just as you have been trained not to present solutions before identifying the prospects' needs, don't try to debrief too early, when the prospect is telling you that you lost the deal.

One final note: oftentimes a salesperson will accept a simple e-mail from the prospect saying something like, "It's not your fault. You did a great job." This is perhaps the worst form of a postloss debrief. For important situations, make sure you request a debrief call. Do not let the process end by e-mail.

Request a Postloss Debrief Call

Once you have learned you lost the deal, here is an example of how to ask for a debrief interview. Again, feel free to fine-tune this into whatever conversational approach you feel best suits your style:

Mr. Prospect, I understand your decision and I respect it. I'm disappointed, because I really wanted to work with you and your company, but I'm not going to try to change your mind. I wish you all the best in the future. If you recall, I had mentioned that my company conducts debriefs at the end of every sales cycle, and you agreed to debrief with me. We do this so we can continuously improve our sales process and product and service offering. Can we set up a time in the next week or so to speak for 15 minutes? It would really be helpful to me. Do you have your calendar handy?

There are many key points to be aware of in the preceding example that will increase your prospect's likelihood of agreeing to a debrief. For one, it is important to let the prospect know you are not going to try to change his mind. This is critical because many people know salespeople who are pushy and won't take "no" for an answer. By letting the prospect know you have accepted the loss and will not try to change his decision, you are putting the prospect at ease. Also, you have let him achieve his main objective for the call (delivering the bad news), and he will be calmed by this. Make sure to let him know you don't like to lose but that you do like to learn as much as possible from every loss.

Additionally, if you have done your homework and asked for the call early in the sales process, you should be well set up to have the prospect grant you an interview. Lastly, it is important to set up the call while you have the prospect on the phone. Asking "Do you have your calendar handy?" is a great sales tactic that really works. Just asking this question immediately makes people look at their calendars and moves them subconsciously toward setting up the call. By asking this question, you take control of the situation.

Do not let the prospect try to give you quick reasons for the loss or try to debrief with you at this point. Remember, he will just be trying to have a quick conversation with you and get you off the phone. Instead, create some space and distance between the loss conversation and your feedback session. This space will help both parties involved. When you create distance, you as the sales rep will be in a more relaxed frame of mind. Additionally, the prospect will be more relaxed because he knows you have already accepted the loss and moved past it.

If the prospect does try to debrief with you instead of setting up a call, tell him you have a questionnaire you use, and you want to prepare your thoughts before the call. Explain to him that you use this process as a tool for self-improvement and that you would really appreciate 15 minutes of his time as a professional courtesy at a later date. Don't forget that reciprocity plays a role here. You can tell him that you and your company put a lot of work into the sales process, and you just want some feedback as a professional courtesy. Additionally, you can set up multiple debriefs if there were multiple people involved in the decision making process.

Here is an example of what to say to a prospect who is trying to debrief with you right away:

> *Mr. Prospect, it would be better if we just set up a time to speak later. I have a questionnaire that we use, and I don't have it in front of me. Also, I would like to take some time to prepare some questions. Do you have any time next Thursday or Friday morning?*

As you can see from this example, another great way to set up a call is by giving the prospect a couple of options for times to speak. This will make her look at her calendar, and she will move toward setting up the call with you.

The best time to schedule a debrief call is one to three weeks after the final decision has been made. If you go beyond this time period, the prospect will most likely have moved on, and she will start to forget crucial differentiation elements of the sales process.

There will be situations in which the prospect is not available or does not answer the phone when you call to debrief. In these cases you will need to use your discretion as to whether the deal was important enough to chase the prospect down to get the feedback. If you really want to speak with the prospect, you will need to get her on the phone again, and then you can conduct the interview with her when you get her live.

In my experience, you should be able to conduct debrief calls with prospects for about 75 percent of your true sales situations. Additionally, you can expect that about one-third of the debriefs will provide very meaningful insights and will significantly help your selling efforts in the future. Another one-third of the calls will provide some meaningful feedback, and the last third will probably not reveal anything signifi-

> **You should be able to conduct debrief calls with prospects for about 75 percent of your true sales situations.**

cant. This is another reason it is important to make postdecision debriefs a regular part of your sales process, because you never know which prospect will provide the best and most meaningful feedback.

Now that we have explored how to set up a debrief call, let's walk through how to act once you have the prospect on the phone for the interview.

HOW TO ACT DURING A POSTDECISION DEBRIEF CALL

Now that you have set up the call, let's review how to act during the debrief to ensure that the prospect feels as comfortable as possible giving you candid feedback. There are many ways to promote candor during a loss debrief, and all of the following ideas will serve to allay the prospect's trepidation about being candid in her remarks and will set the tone of the call as one encouraging detailed responses and extensive feedback.

Begin the Call in a Way That Sets the Tone for Candor

The beginning of the call is very important, because you need to set and control the tone of the discussion. You must make the prospect feel totally comfortable giving you constructive feedback.

In order to do this, you must first convince yourself that you really want this type of feedback. You must be ready and willing to hear the whole truth: the good, the bad, and the ugly. Many salespeople do not seek out this type of criticism, but the best ones always do. Be sure to let the prospect know that you really want the true feedback. It will sting at first, but it will help you grow and win more business in the long run.

Remember, this process is all about helping you increase your close ratio. A necessary step to accomplish this is to track your win rate among sales opportunities. In many ways, your new business win rate tracks with the batting averages of Major League Baseball hitters. If your win ratio is in the 20 to 29 percent range, you may be only an average salesperson. In fact, it has been estimated that 25 percent of all sales are actually made by the customer. So take these factors into account when you look at your win rate. Now, if you have a win rate in the 30 to 40 percent range, then you are a good hitter. If you are winning more than 40 percent of your opportunities, you are a very strong salesperson.

Any way you look at your win rate, there is still plenty of opportunity to learn from your losses. Even a great salesperson who is winning in the 40 percent range is still losing 60 percent of the time. There is a lot of great information that can be gained from prospects to improve your win rate, but you have to want to hear it. Prospects can tell right away if you are not open to getting feedback and therefore will be less forthcoming, so make sure you really want the feedback and that you want to grow.

Also, when you get on the call, make sure the prospect knows that no one will get in trouble or lose his job because of anything that is said. Tell the prospect that no one will be fired as a result of her feedback. Instruct her that your organization encourages this type of dialogue to promote learning and excellence.

Here is an example of how to begin a debrief call:

Ms. Prospect, thank you very much for speaking with me today. I really appreciate it. These feedback calls help us make sure we are working on the right issues instead of having to guess what needs improvement during our sales process and to our products and services. I want to let you know up front that your feedback isn't going to get anyone in trouble. Our company is committed to improving on everything we do, and we view these calls as a critical opportunity to help us achieve that end goal. So please be as candid as possible; you will not hurt my feelings with anything you have to say. I am totally open to any constructive feedback because ultimately it will help me do my job better.

> **Prospects can tell right away if you are not open to getting feedback and therefore will be less forthcoming, so make sure you really want the feedback.**

By properly framing the discussion, you are making the prospect feel comfortable sharing her honest opinion. You are also letting her know you are expecting to get some constructive criticism. This is very different from how most conversations go. It is very rare that people seek out constructive feedback on themselves, so you must frame the discussion so the prospect understands that you are not simply looking to identify things you did well but that you are very interested in the areas where you and your company can improve.

Some prospects may ask at the beginning of the debrief call how this information will be used. Let them know that the information will be used by you primarily to enhance your selling efforts in the future. However, you should also let them know that if they provide feedback about your company's products or services, you may share it with others in your company. If the prospect does not want any information shared with anyone else, tell her it is not a problem and agree to keep all the feedback confidential (and make a note to yourself to make sure you actually do it!).

Remove Any Salesmanship from the Conversation

* *Take responsibility.* The first step to making sure you act professionally on debrief calls is to make sure you take personal responsibility for losing. If you are still of the mind-set that anyone else is to blame for losing the deal, you need to change that attitude quickly. In all of my years interacting with thousands of sales professionals, I have learned that the best and most successful salespeople always take personal responsibility for themselves and their losses (and they always want to know what they can do better because they are winners). If you are still blaming prospects for your losses, this will come across in

> The first step to making sure you act professionally on debrief calls is to make sure you take personal responsibility for losing.

your loss debriefs, so watch yourself and take responsibility for the loss and apologize for any sales issues during the sales process. Put your ego away and be as positive as possible.

If you do this, you will quickly find that prospects will become more receptive and will in turn want to help you out by giving you information to improve yourself and your company. As I mentioned earlier, if you truly want feedback and you also take responsibility, you will be amazed by how much people have to offer to help you improve. So few people actually strive to get criticism that when you come across as someone who is willing to listen, most people find it refreshing.

- *Don't get defensive or angry.* As we reviewed in Chapters 2 and 3, when you lose a deal, it is very easy to get defensive or angry at the situation. You must make sure that when you are conducting debriefs, you do not come across as defensive (and of course, never show any anger). You might think all this goes without saying, but I have seen many salespeople get angry and emotional at prospects on debrief calls. Anger, in any situation, cuts off your options for the future. Once you get angry at a prospect for losing a deal, you have most certainly killed your chances of ever being invited to bid on other business in the future. You have also made a bad impression for your company, and bad impressions can spread just as fast as (if not faster than) positive impressions.

- *Don't debate with the prospect.* You must also never debate with the prospect on the debrief call. The minute you try to debate a topic or discuss any feedback the prospect is giving you, he will cease giving you constructive feedback. Prospects simply don't want to argue with you. Therefore, you must remain as neutral as possible on the call at all times to ensure that the prospect feels he can be candid. Just listen and don't comment or make judgments on what is being said (the time for that is later). Remember, the prospect's perception of the situation is just as important as the facts.

> The minute you try to debate a topic or discuss any feedback the prospect is giving you, he will cease giving you constructive feedback.

An example of debating would be any situation where you start to question the prospect's feedback. Here is an example of a dialogue in which a salesperson can appear to be debating with the prospect:

Prospect: "Your company's technology could not do X, Y, and Z and therefore wasn't a good fit for our needs. The competitor's technology could do X, Y, and Z, and that is why we chose them."

Salesperson: "You know Mr. Prospect, our technology actually can do X, Y, and Z, and we went over those areas during the presentation . . ."

This type of situation occurs often; you lose a sale over a feature the prospect believes your company could not provide. Instead of acting defensively, realize that perhaps the real issue was that you did not present your capabilities as clearly as the competition. Therefore, a better response with less debate would be:

Salesperson: "You know, Mr. Prospect, I obviously didn't do a good job at presenting our technology capabilities, and I take responsibility for that. Our system can do all of those things. What could I have done better in the presentation to bring those points out and make things more clear in my future presentations?"

By phrasing your response this way, you are not debating at all with the prospect; as a result, he will be more likely to give you constructive feedback. At this point, he may tell you that you should have spent more time on the technology portion of the presentation, or he may tell you your demonstration lacked excitement, or that you appeared less knowledgeable than the competition, etc. Either way, by taking responsibility and not debating, you will be much more likely to get to the real issues.

Don't try to "resell" the prospect. Avoid trying to resell the prospect on your product or service. This is another common problem for salespeople when they conduct debriefs. This is certainly understandable because salespeople are trained at objection handling; when they hear a prospect saying something about their products or about themselves, salespeople will typically begin handling the situation as if it were an objection that occurred during the sales process. This is problematic because if prospects feel you are trying to sell them again, they become frustrated and will inevitably withhold critical information. Make sure this does not happen to you subconsciously.

So remember, take responsibility, don't get defensive or angry, and never debate or try to resell the prospect. If you conduct yourself professionally during the debrief, you will have accomplished two very important things: (1) you will have gained valuable knowledge about what you can improve in the future, which will help you win more business, and (2) you will leave the prospect with a feeling of goodwill that may make her more likely to call you in future business situations. Don't underestimate the power of future business opportunities. Make sure you act professionally, because you never know what can happen a year or two later.

I am not blaming salespeople for acting in any of these manners; many of these behaviors are natural reactions that come with the territory of the sales profession (no pun intended). When you work hard to win business, it can be very difficult to detach yourself from the situation and learn from it (especially when your income is depending on it). I have personally experienced all of these issues in my own selling situations. Sometimes it has taken me six months to one year to accept and fully realize the true reasons for losing a deal. Be sure to compensate for these areas as best as you can when you are debriefing with prospects, and try to act as professionally as possible; it will pay big dividends over time.

Consider Having Someone Else Conduct the Debrief Call for You

As you can see from the last section, there are many things a salesperson must be aware of when conducting a debrief call. Additionally, it is common knowledge that prospects tend to grade the person to whom they are speaking higher than anyone else involved in the sales process. This is human nature, and there is not much you can do about it. For example, if there were three people involved in the sales presentation, the sales rep who conducts the interview will most likely get the highest score from the prospect out of courtesy.

To rectify this situation, consider having someone else conduct the interviews for you, particularly in larger deals or for important losses. By having someone who was not involved with the prospect during the sales process conduct the call, you will be able to remove any "salesy" and bias elements from the call.

There are many options available for others to conduct the calls on your behalf. For instance, you may have an inside sales rep or an assistant who handles certain functions for you. Once you've designed the questionnaire, you can easily have this person speak with prospects. However, make sure that this person is articulate and possesses strong phone skills, someone who can get a prospect on the phone and engage her in a conversation.

Another option is to have someone from your marketing or product area conduct the debrief calls. This process sometimes gets picked up by marketing or product development because prospect bids lost and bids won feedback also benefits these areas. For instance, win/loss debriefs often uncover specific product or service issues that would be critical for the product and marketing areas to analyze. Also, competitive intelligence can be gained during postdecision interviews, which can help your company develop competitive advantages.

Lastly, there are many independent third-party market research firms that perform this type of research for sales teams. However, these types of engagements are usually applied to the whole sales team versus one individual sales rep. An independent third party will always be able to get the best and most candid information from prospects. However, do not let this deter you from learning how to better conduct your own debriefs. As we have shown, most salespeople approach this situation in unproductive ways. By learning how to conduct the process correctly, you can drastically improve the amount and quality of feedback you gather and ultimately increase your win rate.

Now that we have reviewed how to correctly set up a postloss debrief and how to conduct yourself in a professional manner on the call, let's go over some proven interview techniques that will allow you to dig deeper into critical issues and gather more valuable information.

PROVEN INTERVIEW TECHNIQUES TO GATHER THE MOST VALUABLE INFORMATION

Following is a series of proven interview techniques guaranteed to make the most of the time you spend with the prospect on the phone. Each of these ideas will serve as a building block off the questionnaire you have already designed. Remember, the questionnaire is just a starting point for the discussion. You must implement the following probing techniques in order to dig deeper and get the prospect past surface issues.

It is important to note that if you don't act professionally and follow the basics we explored in the last section, the upcoming techniques will be of no use to you. This is why I have placed them after the section on how to act on the call.

Take Notes

At the beginning of the call, tell the prospect you are going to be taking notes. This lets the prospect know that what she is saying is important, and it is a psychological fact that people tend to talk and reveal more when they know that someone is taking notes. It makes them feel important. You should take notes during the sales process, and you should also take notes on the debrief call. Make sure that you leave plenty of room in your questionnaire for note taking.

Just as your opening remarks for the interview let the prospect know you are looking for constructive feedback, taking notes also reinforces the fact that you are looking for the prospect to open up and talk.

Lastly, taking comprehensive notes will be critical for you in the future as you begin to track your trends for winning and losing deals. It will be impossible to remember everything the prospect said, so good note taking is essential. This will also help you if you are fortunate enough to engage with the prospect on other business. If you perform a successful and professional debrief, the chances of your being asked to bid on future opportunities from the prospect is likely to increase substantially.

Probe for Specifics

It is also very important to continually probe for specifics during the debrief call. Don't just let the prospect give you a couple of sentences on a topic. Encourage the prospect to elaborate. Ask questions like,

"How do you mean?" or "Can you tell me more about that point?" This will show that you are truly interested in hearing the truth, and it will uncover the real issues behind the reasons for loss. Keep probing.

For example, if the prospect says your price was higher than the competition's, don't be afraid to ask, "By how much?" or ask for a percentage differential. If the prospect says he liked the technology of a competitor better than your company's technology, ask for specific examples of features that stood out.

> Encourage the prospect to elaborate. Ask questions like, "How do you mean?" or "Can you tell me more about that point?"

Another great question to ask is, "If you were to buy our product at some point in the future, what would cause you to do it at that time?" Very often, this probing question will reveal the true reasons for loss.

Use Silence to Get the Prospect Talking

Another great interview technique is to use silence as a way of getting the prospect to talk. Similar to during the sales process, you want to let the prospect do most of the talking on this call. The selling takes place when you are talking, but the prospect "buys" during the moments of silence you give her to mull things over during your presentation. In short, prospects need time to process information; this is no different in the debrief process. Allowing for silence is a very valuable tool in your probing arsenal. When you let someone sit in silence, you are allowing her to think about how to give you the best and most constructive feedback.

Whatever the Prospect Talks About the Most Is Important

Whatever the prospect talks about most on the debrief call is what was most important to him during the sales process. Therefore, if the prospect goes on and on about how polished, prepared, and customized the other sales team was, it means that that was important to the buyer. It also means you were not as polished, prepared, and customized. So at the end of your debrief call, reflect on the things the prospect kept coming back to during the interview. These topics were the key criteria in his decision making process.

If you are successful in getting the prospect to talk about the things that were truly important to him, many times you will find that you cannot follow your debrief questionnaire perfectly. Often, the prospect will begin talking and you will find yourself touching on many different subjects all at once. Don't try to force the prospect to follow your agenda; just let him speak and fill in the sections as you go. Follow his lead, and once he is done, circle back around and make sure you have raised all your survey questions.

Listen to Stories

Listening for stories is another way to pick up on messages that the prospect is trying to tell you. We all communicate through stories, and whenever you hear a story, either during or after the sales process, the prospect is trying to tell you something. No one shares a story without trying to convey a message, so listen closely and take notes. You may not be able to fully understand what the prospect is trying to tell you, and you may need to reflect on it later, but pay attention. Hidden within the story is a message to you, so make sure your ears perk up when a prospect starts telling a story.

Listen to How the Prospect Talks About the Winning Salesperson

Just like when the prospect tells a story, getting the prospect to talk about the winning salesperson or company is valuable. Pay attention to what the prospect says about the winning rep, as this will likely provide invaluable insights for your own personal improvement. If the prospect talks about the winning sales rep and says something like, "He really clicked with us, and we felt like he understood our needs," then that means you did not have as good a rapport with the prospect or audience and that you were not as in tune with what the buyer was looking for. Ask follow-up questions such as, "How did he achieve that?" or "What type of person was the winning sales rep?"

Neutralize Your Questioning Disposition

In *Secrets of Question Based Selling,* Thomas Freese (Naperville, Ill: Sourcebooks, Inc., 2000, pp. 147–158) highlights how to neutralize your questioning disposition. This is a valuable tool you can use not only during your sales process but also in asking questions and debriefing with prospects. He explains that most salespeople tend to ask questions in a hopeful manner, which means that you show the prospect in your questioning that you have hopes for getting positive information and ultimately closing the deal. However, this is problematic not only during the sales process but especially when trying to conduct a candid debrief. Hopeful questioning steers prospects into giving a certain type of information that may be more guarded and less truthful.

For example, if you ask a question like, "Did you like our presentation?" you are asking that question in a hopeful way that directs prospects to give you more positive feedback. However, the reverse actually happens. When you ask a hopeful question, you actually tend to get less accurate information, and, in fact, the answers tend to be more conservative than uplifting.

So how do you fix this problem? The answer is to add a neutralizing subquestion at the end of your question. This can simply be done by adding the words "or not" at the end of these types of questions. So you could ask, "Did you like our presentation, or not?" By asking the question in this way, you are actually putting the prospect at ease and letting her know you are comfortable with hearing negative feedback as well as positive critiques. When you do this, you are actually more likely to get true and honest feedback. So if she really liked your presentation, she will make an effort to let you honestly know how much she liked what you did. However, if she thought your presentation skills needed work, she will be much more likely to reveal your areas for improvement.

By the way, adding a neutralizing disposition works in any situation, not just sales. So if you want to get feedback on the tie or dress you are wearing, ask, "Do you like this tie or not?" or "Do you like this dress or not?" By asking the question this way, you are allowing the respondent to feel as though she can be candid, something people rarely do. You are providing her with options because you are open to either path of feedback.

To Ask Tough Questions, Start with a Humbling Disclaimer

In *Secrets of Question Based Selling,* Thomas Freese further cites that in many sales situations, there will most certainly be difficult and tough questions that you may want to ask the prospect. For example, there may have been something you said or did during the sales process that you want to understand the full impact of. The best way to ask these tough questions is to start with some type of a humbling disclaimer. Start with something like, "I'm not sure how to ask this, but . . ." or "At the risk of getting myself in trouble, would you mind if I . . ."

Humbling disclaimers serve to soften the tough question, and, more importantly, they give the prospect the opportunity to rescue you, which is a part of human nature. Often before you even get to the real question, the prospect will rescue you by saying, "No, no, ask me anything." By asking questions in this way, it also serves to add humility to the conversation, and it really softens up the dialogue. Prospects love humility, and it allows them to be more forthcoming with information.

Lastly, as we discussed in the last chapter, the time to ask these tough questions is toward the end of the debrief call because at this point, you have most likely already warmed up the prospect and gotten him talking. Use the last section of your questionnaire to insert these types of tough questions into your dialogue, and if need be insert a humbling disclaimer.

Verify All the Reasons for Winning and Losing

One final technique to implement when concluding a postdecision debrief is to verify all the key discussion points with the prospect before you end the call. This will not only show the prospect that you listened but also will allow her to correct you if you are off in any areas. Also, don't be afraid of making a mistake in front of the prospect. Remember, you have nothing to lose at this point, but you do have a lot to gain from totally understanding why you win and lose.

Once you are done verifying everything with the prospect, ask her this final verification question: "Have I missed anything?" Another variation of this question is "What else should I be asking?" These are great questions to ask at the end of an interview (and also at the end of any sales meeting). These questions allow the prospect to think of anything she might have missed, and if she did, the prospect now has an opportunity to go over it with you. If nothing has been missed in the discussion, these questions allow the prospect to verify that you covered and understand everything and they also show the prospect that you are thorough. Most of the time the prospect will say, "No, I think we've covered everything." However, I have learned that you can sometimes gain some really telling insights by asking these questions. You will find that prospects are impressed with this type of question.

CHAPTER WRAP-UP

Each section in this chapter is critical for conducting successful prospect debrief calls. By implementing the process of correctly setting up debrief calls, you will be making a significant and needed enhancement to your sales process. By learning how to act on these calls and how to probe skillfully into significant issues, you will unlock a vast source of prospect information and knowledge that will allow for a continuous cycle of feedback and sales improvement. This process will ultimately increase your new business win rate for years to come.

Now that you have learned how to conduct yourself on postdecision debrief calls, in the next chapter we will address how to identify and analyze trends in your conversations.

CHAPTER SUMMARY

How to Set Up a Postdecision Debrief Call

* Get approval for the postdecision debrief early in the sales process.
* Ask for permission to debrief with the prospect after you have built rapport, identified the needs of the prospect, and begun presenting your solution.
* Do not debrief when you first hear from the prospect that you lost the deal.
* Ask for a debrief interview after you have accepted the loss, and let the prospect know you will not try to change his decision.
* The best way to set up a call is to ask the prospect, "Do you have your calendar handy?"

How to Act During a Prospect Debrief Call

* Start the call in a positive manner that sets the tone for candor.
* Make sure you really want to hear constructive feedback (the prospect will be able to tell if you don't).
* Let the prospect know that no one will get in trouble and the call is not a witch hunt.
* Take responsibility for everything that occurred during the sales process.
* Don't get defensive or angry, don't debate with the prospect, and don't try to resell the prospect.

Proven Interview Techniques to Gather the Most Valuable Information

* Take notes to make the prospect feel important and to keep her talking.
* Probe for specifics. Ask "How do you mean?" or "Say more."
* Use silence to get the prospect talking and to create space for the prospect to provide constructive feedback.
* Understand that whatever the prospect talks about most was important to her during the sales process.
* Listen for stories; they convey important messages and feedback.
* To learn more about your selling deficiencies, listen to how the prospect talks about the winning sales rep.
* Neutralize your questioning disposition by adding "or not" at the end of relevant questions.
* When asking tough questions, start with a humbling disclaimer.

Identify and Analyze Your Win/Loss Trends

Now that you have designed your own customized postdecision debrief questionnaire and learned how to skillfully debrief with prospects to get more actionable information, the next step in the process is to identify and analyze the trends within your own feedback.

In the first part of this chapter, I will teach you a three-step process for analyzing prospect feedback so that you can act on identified trends pertaining to your sales performance, your company's products or services, and the things your competitors are doing to successfully compete against you. The second part of the chapter will show you why it is so important to discuss the feedback with other sales team personnel so that you can gain a better understanding of the data.

Let's first explore a simple way to identify and analyze trends from prospect feedback.

HOW TO IDENTIFY AND ANALYZE TRENDS FROM YOUR POSTDECISION DEBRIEFS

Effectively identifying trends involves an easy three-step process. Step 1 is to conduct enough interviews for a representative sample. Step 2 is to analyze your results in aggregate to identify your strengths and weaknesses at a high level. Step 3 is to create a two-page dashboard of your strengths and weaknesses with a specific analysis of each area.

Step 1: Obtain a Representative Data Set

Identifying trends in your feedback is relatively simple, and you will find that you will naturally begin to act on the ongoing feedback. However, you should make sure you perform a sufficient number of debriefs to be able to truly identify trends.

There is no magic number of debriefs you should conduct in order to have a representative sample, as the target number depends on how many sales situations you enter into each year; this number varies by individual, company, and industry. For example, if you are involved in only 10 sales situations per year and you conduct 10 debriefs, you will have a sufficient sample. However, if you are involved in 75 sales situations per year, you would likely want more interviews to ensure a representative data set.

As a starting point, a simple rule of thumb is for you to get feedback on 30 of your sales situations. If you are not in 30 situations per year, then get as many as you can. You should also make sure you are conducting debriefs for true sales situations in which you have made an actual sales presentation to your prospect, as opposed to "cold calls" or situations in which you were only peripherally involved. Focusing on true sales situations will eliminate "noise" from the data and will yield the most meaningful feedback on all aspects of your sales process.

> There is no magic number of debriefs you should conduct in order to have a representative sample, as the target number depends on how many sales situations you enter into each year; this number varies by individual, company, and industry.

Additionally, you should strive to either have an equal number of win debriefs versus loss debriefs (roughly 15 wins and 15 losses), or to focus more on your losses and perform a 60/40 loss/win split, respectively (18 losses and 12 wins). While these are guidelines, you should really make a concerted effort to debrief with all of your prospects postdecision, and you should build the discipline to make this process an integral part of your sales cycle. The more you perform this exercise, the more you will learn. Once you've performed enough debriefs, you will be ready to start identifying trends and acting on the feedback.

> A simple rule of thumb is for you to get feedback on 30 of your sales situations. If you are not in 30 situations per year, then get as many as you can.

Although I have given you some rough parameters with respect to the number of debriefs you should conduct, don't worry too much about what sample size you need in order to analyze your results. As long as you begin following the program outlined in this book, you will be able to improve your sales effectiveness and will be miles ahead of most other salespeople. Whether you apply all of the ideas in this book or just a few, you will be moving in the right direction with respect to debriefing in a more productive way.

Step 2: "Roll Up" Your Responses

Once you have conducted a good sample of debrief interviews, you are ready to begin analyzing the trends. At this point, you should sit down with a journal or spreadsheet and tally up all the feedback you have received from prospects. Depending on your industry and sales process, you will be able to break out the data into several different areas. The way to do this is to examine your notes from each interview and identify the three to five most frequently mentioned strengths and weaknesses. The best place to start is with the questions that explicitly ask for your top strengths and weaknesses. That said, you should not discount feedback from other sections of the interview, as additional strengths and weaknesses can sometimes be drawn out of a prospect during different sections of the interview.

Here are five broad categories in which you can begin to categorize your prospect feedback:

1. Sales performance
   a. Your sales performance
   b. Sales presentation

     c. Sales materials (e.g., proposal/RFP response, presentation handouts)

     d. The sales performance of others on your team with whom you sell (if applicable)

     e. The sales performance of any intermediaries through which you sell (if applicable)

     f. Site visit (if applicable)

2. Product or service issues

     a. Strengths or deficiencies in your company's existing suite

     b. Product gaps/missing features

     c. Technology (if applicable)

3. Client service/customer support

4. Price

5. Brand image of your firm

     a. Name brand recognition

     b. Commitment to your marketplace

     c. Perceptions of your company's brand/reputation

Depending on the industry in which you sell, these parameters may change, but most of these areas will be applicable to your sales process. In certain cases, you will find that some areas come out as both a strength and a weakness. This is not uncommon and is often an indication of an inconsistency in your sales process.

Once you have tallied up how many prospects offered positive and negative feedback in each of these areas, create a percentage ranking of each area. You do this by counting how many positive or negative mentions occurred in each category and dividing the number by the base number of debrief interviews you conducted. For example, if you conducted 15 bids lost debriefs and 5 loss prospects mentioned a specific product or service feature as an area for improvement or reason for loss, you would conclude that 33 percent of bids lost prospects cited this as an issue (5/15 = 33 percent). In order to gain a clear understanding of which prospect perceptions drive losses versus wins, you should break this data out separately by both bids lost and bids won.

Here is an example of what your analysis should look like at this point:

TOP STRENGTHS

* **Product/service capabilities.** Mentioned as a top strength by 64 percent of bids won and 11 percent of bids lost.
* **Sales rep/sales team.** Mentioned by 57 percent of bids won prospects and 33 percent of bids lost.
* **Competitiveness of fees.** Mentioned by 50 percent of bids won and 33 percent of bids lost.
* **Client service.** Mentioned by 43 percent of bids won and 33 percent of bids lost.

TOP AREAS FOR IMPROVEMENT

* **Sales presentation/sales team.** Mentioned as a top weakness by 48 percent of bids lost prospects and 43 percent of bids won prospects.
* **Technology.** Mentioned by 41 percent of bids lost and 18 percent of bids won.
* **Brand image.** Mentioned by 30 percent of bids lost prospects.
* **Site visit.** Mentioned by 20 percent of bids lost prospects.

Once you get to this point, the data should be starting to highlight trends, and you should be getting a clearer picture of your strengths and weaknesses. Just use your best judgment as to where each feedback point should be placed.

Step 3: Create a Two-Page Dashboard That Explains Why You Win and Lose

Once you have tallied up the responses at a high level, the next step is to create definitions of what prospects are saying within each category. For example, if prospects are citing your company's brand image as an issue, define the issues in the words of your prospects (such as limited name recognition, weak perceptions based on marketplace rumors, or a perception that your company is not committed to the marketplace).

Another example would be feedback on your company's products or services. Be sure to assess what the issues are. Are prospects mentioning a lack of specific product features, or are they citing that your products are not as streamlined or easy to use as the competition's products?

With respect to sales performance, try to identify specific areas where you are strong and weak. Is it your preparation abilities, are you not customizing your pitch, do prospects have issues with your team selling approach, or do they view your site visits negatively?

Make sure you can clearly articulate three to five descriptions within each high-level category that explain specifically what prospects are saying. Ultimately the goal is for you to be able to write out in two pages why you are winning and why you are losing.

Following is an expanded example of the type of analysis you should be able to perform if you approach this process correctly. This example is from the financial services industry for a salesperson who is selling 401(k) services.

TOP STRENGTHS

- **Investment capabilities.** Mentioned as a top strength by 58 percent of bids won and 11 percent bids lost (flexibility, wide variety of funds, investment planning tools, Morningstar reports).
- **Sales rep/sales team.** Mentioned by 48 percent of bids won prospects interviewed and 18 percent of bids lost (knowledgeable, experienced, prepared, quality of relationship managers, chemistry/fit with team, cohesive team, demonstrated passion/enthusiasm).
- **Employee education and communications.** Mentioned by 36 percent of bids won and 20 percent of bids lost (high-quality personnel, customized and high-quality materials, effective online tools and information, creative approach, multiple mediums—mail, Webinars, and face-to-face meetings).

- **Pricing.** Mentioned by 36 percent of bids won and 18 percent of bids lost (pricing in line with competition, willingness to negotiate, transparency).
- **Client service.** Mentioned by 32 percent of bids won and 16 percent of bids lost (high-quality/knowledgeable personnel, willingness to customize/flexibility, strong industry rankings/survey results, favorable references).

TOP AREAS FOR IMPROVEMENT

- **Sales presentation/sales team.** Mentioned as a top weakness by 56 percent of bids lost and 43 percent of bids won prospects interviewed (failure to address prospects' key issues, lack of customization, lack of preparedness, issues with key sales team members, team does not come across as a cohesive unit, competition demonstrated higher desire for business).
- **Web site/technology.** Mentioned by 48 percent of bids lost (capabilities lag competition, missing bells and whistles, look and feel, ease of navigation, inability to include outside assets/accounts, demo not provided).
- **Fit with client service team.** Mentioned by 37 percent of bids lost prospects (key personnel/day-to-day contact not in attendance at presentation, lack of chemistry, weak presentation skills compared to competition, issues with personnel resulted in weaker perceptions of the company's client service quality).
- **Site visit.** Mentioned by 29 percent of total bids lost prospects and by 66 percent of bids lost prospects who had a site visit (concerns surrounding ability to adequately service the plan sponsor, physical appearance of the building/location, mix of personnel present for visit).

Another way to analyze the data is to create a quantitative ranking of your benchmarking/assessment of the competition questions.

Begin by assigning point values to each of your benchmarking questions (5 points for "Much better than the winning firm," 3 points for "Equal to the winning firm," etc.). Then take an average score for all your benchmarking attributes and rank them from top to bottom. This will allow you to compare your performance against the competition to identify relative strengths and weaknesses, and it's a useful addition to your dashboard. Here is an example of how this might look:

Criteria	Average rating
Brand/reputation	4.26
My ability to make you feel you would be valued as a client	4.21
Client service	4.15
My responsiveness	4.07
My ability to understand your unique needs and offer solutions	4.04
Presentation materials	4.01
Pricing	4.00
Proposal/RFP response	3.91
My overall preparedness	3.75
My presentation	3.66
My product/industry knowledge	3.50
Customization of the presentation	3.48
Technological capabilities	2.98
Cohesiveness of our sales team	2.39

It takes time, discipline, and consistent tracking of trending data to ultimately determine what needs to be changed or improved during your sales process. If you commit to conducting this research on an ongoing basis and incorporating it into your routine, you will easily be able to more accurately identify why you are winning and losing.

After you have been rigorously tracking your wins and losses for a while, you will also begin to get a better sense of recurring patterns of prospect objections. Once you understand the full range of objections, you will be in a much better position to handle them during the sales process. You will also be better able to create effective sales materials and customize your pitch. You will get better at anticipating when future prospects are likely to have similar reservations to past prospects, and this will allow you to be more proactive and convincing in your objection handling.

Solid preparation always leads to stronger performance. When you take the time to fully debrief with prospects and learn all the reasons you win and lose, you will not only be better able to handle objections, but you will also feel more comfortable and experienced during the process. When you look and feel more confident in handling prospect objections, you will exude a sense of calm toward the prospect. Prospects will read this positively and will feel better about deciding to buy from you.

Once you have aggregated your data for the first time, you should make sure you continue this process on a regular basis. I recommend analyzing your interviews every six months and updating your two-page dashboard. Alternatively, you may choose to analyze your trends on an ongoing basis and update your dashboard as you go. Either way, you should keep a copy of each subsequent two-page dashboard and review how the data changes over time.

Once you have your two-page description of exactly why you win and lose, you will be in a great position to take this data to others in your company and share your insights with them. This is a critical part of the process, because you may often find that you are too close to the situation to gather insights on how you can improve. By sharing this information with a wider audience, you will gain valuable knowledge as you leverage the brainpower of other experienced individuals. In the next section, we'll review who you should share this feedback with and how to do it. This is a powerful next step in allowing you to fully scrutinize the feedback you receive from prospects.

ANALYZE TRENDS WITH OTHER SALES TEAM MEMBERS

Now that you have created a written assessment of why you are winning and losing, the next step is to discuss the results with other parties who are involved (directly or indirectly) in your sales process. These include:

- Your sales manager
- Other people with whom you sell (such as team members, client service people, technical personnel, or any intermediaries/consultants)
- Other top producing members of your sales team

It is absolutely critical for you to share and discuss this data with others. Don't just hold on to the information yourself, for you will limit your ability to truly understand the issues, and it will hold you back from improving your sales performance.

Let's review how to analyze your data by commissioning feedback from other stakeholders on your sales team.

Gather Feedback from Your Sales Manager or Sales Mentor

One valuable way to improve your sales effectiveness is by spending time with your sales manager or sales mentor to review your prospect feedback on why you win and lose. Print out your two-page dashboard and show it to your sales manager to discuss all the reasons why you are winning and losing. You will find that this conversation will be beneficial in helping you better understand and analyze the results. Ask your sales manager for her opinion of what you are finding, and let her offer solutions about how you can mitigate your deficiencies and play up your strengths. Brainstorming on ways to improve your sales efforts with your sales manager is an efficient means for maximizing future sales performance. Most sales managers have a lot of knowledge about best sales practices in your marketplace, so use them as a guide. Your organization and commitment to improvement is also likely to impress your sales manager.

Approaching your sales manager for this type of advice will help you build your relationship. Most sales managers appreciate being approached for advice, especially about ways that you can improve your performance. As Benjamin Franklin once said, "If you ever want to make a friend, ask them to do you a favor." When you develop your relationship in this way, you are not only setting up a process for getting feedback and support from your manager, but she will also learn to like you more. As the quote says, people are more likely to like you if they do you a favor. This is a win-win. You win because you'll become a better salesperson, and your sales manager will like you more. Sales managers win because they feel helpful, and it should ultimately make them more money (since they typically do well when their salespeople do well). Your feedback will also help your sales manager better understand what she needs to lobby for (to senior management) with respect to sales process modifications and product or service changes.

In the corporate world, it has always been challenging to find mentors among senior management or to make time to mentor others. This is why you need to seek it out. People often complain that they do not receive enough training or guidance from their managers, but this is really the individual's responsibility and not the company's. If you want to improve your performance, there are plenty of ways you can do it. For example, you can read books, you can attend seminars, and you can find mentors. All of these things are within your control. Therefore, instead of waiting for someone to come to you and offer help, go to them and ask for advice. Trust me, very few people in your career are going to come to you looking to help you out. You must take control of this situation.

I've personally worked with many salespeople who did not ask for much advice from their sales managers. Whether it was because they did not have a good relationship with their managers or perhaps they felt that they could figure everything out on their own, this behavior worked to their detriment. Also, just because you might feel that your sales manager is not a good manager, don't make the assumption that she doesn't know how to sell. The skills required to be a great manager and a great salesperson are not the same.

By collaborating with your sales manager on why you are winning and losing, you will unleash a rewarding dialogue and bonding experience, and you will have a powerful way to leverage your sales manager's knowledge of the sales process. Two heads are better than one.

Gather Feedback from Others Involved in Your Sales Process

You should also perform this same process with colleagues who may be involved in your sales process (such as other sales presentation team members, client service people, product experts, technical personnel, or intermediaries/consultants). These are people who may or may not be "salespeople" but who are instrumental in your sales process and presentations. Take your two-page dashboard and review it with each player who may be involved in your sales presentations. Get their thoughts and feedback.

This process can make them better, because you may uncover action items for them to work on as well. For example, you might have received feedback that your sales team is not presenting in a cohesive manner. You also might have learned some things that the competition is doing to sell more effectively than you and your team. Whatever the feedback, discussing it with others involved in your sales process will open up a dialogue about how to improve.

> Take your two-page dashboard and review it with each player who may be involved in your sales presentations. Get their thoughts and feedback.

You should also make sure you debrief with these types of stakeholders directly after each sales presentation. There are three key questions that salespeople should ask other presentation team members after a sales presentation:

1. What three things do you think I (or we) did well?
2. What three things do you think I (or we) could improve on?
3. What is the one thing that I (or we) didn't do that you'd like to see me/us do?

By using this simple technique, you will be able to easily approach anyone who is involved in the sales process with you. This three-question strategy works best if applied right after you are involved in a sales situation. For example, if you leave a prospect's office and you conducted the sales presentation with someone else from your company (or with some other third party), take time to ask them these three questions right after you are done with the meeting.

This strategy is a formulaic way to gather constructive feedback and also to debrief with your counterpart(s) on all the different areas of your sales presentation. Often, you might feel good about a particular point in the presentation while your colleague might feel that you could have done better. Also, some people are better at reading people or prospects than others, and their opinions might be more insightful.

This process also works both ways. If the other people with whom you sell begin to see that you are open to constructive feedback, they may decide to partake in this exercise. For example, you may have to sell with someone who has trouble in certain areas of the presentation, and it may be hard for you to give criticism if the other person is not open to it. By showing them that you are willing to accept feedback (both from prospects and from others on your sales team), they may become more inclined to become part of the feedback process. Ultimately, this will raise the performance level of everyone on your sales team.

After you have debriefed with other team members, you should also always take a few minutes to review in your own mind how the meeting went. This is critical because if there are things you could have done better, you will need to make sure that you address them later in the sales process. By using the above approach, you will flesh out the things you do well and the things you need to work on. You can also overlay these discussions against your two-page dashboard, and this will allow you to put your sales meetings in a better context.

Whether you reflect on your own or in a group with other sales team members, this is a valuable part of the sales process for two reasons:

1. *It can be hard to realize how things are going during a live sales presentation.* When you are presenting, you don't have time to reflect on the big picture and what might be going on in the prospect's mind. You are very often thinking of the next part of your presentation or are already fielding

questions from the prospect. By replaying the meeting in your mind, you give yourself valuable time to process everything that occurred during the sales call.

2. *Taking time to reflect after a sales call is valuable because it will help you highlight things that you can clarify with the prospect in your next interaction.* When you are in a meeting, you may lack the technical knowledge to answer a particularly detailed prospect question. When you take time to reflect after the call, you will be in a better position to recall any points of clarification that you need to follow up on or proactively bring up in your next prospect interaction.

Don't make the mistake of quickly moving on to your next sales situation and forgetting to take time to debrief with yourself and with your team. Often you will find two or three items that you could have improved upon during each sales call, and if you overlay this information with your two-page dashboard, you will be in a much better position to put everything in context. If you aren't learning a few things from each sales call, you might not be reflecting enough. When you are in front of a prospect for an hour or more, it is almost impossible for there not to be something that does not go as well as you would have liked. You can always improve.

Gather Input from Other Top Producing Members of Your Sales Team

One final group of people who can be instrumental for acquiring feedback and insights is other top salespeople in your field. Make sure that as you grow in your career, you spend time with the stars of your team. Ask them why they win and lose and what they have done to become successful. Bounce off of them the insights you've learned from prospects and get their opinions. The more time you spend with people who are effective at selling, the better salesperson you will become. You are probably already having these types of discussions with others on your sales team; however, by using your two-page dashboard as a basis for the conversation, you will have more detailed discussions and acquire more insights.

Also, if you want to really take what you have learned to the next level, consider spending time with the poor performers or new salespeople on your team. During this time, you can educate them on what you've learned

> **Spend time with the stars of your team. Ask them why they win and lose and what they have done to become successful.**

and the strategies you're implementing. This will not only help them become better performers but will help you because as you teach them, it will reinforce what you've learned and help you better understand why you win and lose. You may even want to train others on your team about how to conduct win/loss reviews so they too can learn how to improve their close rate.

CHAPTER WRAP-UP

There are many benefits to identifying the trends and analyzing the results of your postdecision conversations. Over time, you will realize things that you did not notice when you debriefed with each prospect individually. When you aggregate your feedback, you will be in a better position to understand the big picture and gather insights that will help you improve your sales performance. Also, by committing to typing out a two-page document and putting your analysis in writing, you will find that this process crystallizes your thinking and helps you fully define your strengths and areas for improvement.

This process also lends itself to having detailed discussions with others on your sales team. Discussing what you learned in your postdecision debriefs with other members of your sales team is a key part of the process. Taking time to bounce your prospect feedback off other sales team members and sales managers will help you make sense of the information and will allow you to better formulate what changes you need to make to your sales process. You will also help others on your sales team improve their sales performance because they will learn from your feedback. Remember, others on your sales team are likely struggling with the same issues you are, so don't be shy to start a discussion on the topic.

This chapter marks the end of Part 2 of this book. In Part 1 we explored the benefits of win/loss analysis and the potential challenges of successful postdecision debriefs. In Part 2 we showed you techniques on how to conduct the process more efficiently by teaching you how to design a questionnaire, how to conduct more thorough interviews, and how to identify and analyze trends.

In the final section of this book, we will explore how to leverage what you learned in the first two sections and take action on your results so you can improve your close rate and win more business.

CHAPTER SUMMARY

Identify and Analyze Trends

- Conduct enough postdecision debriefs with prospects to provide you with a representative sample.
- Conduct approximately half of your debrief interviews with bids won and half with bids lost.
- Aggregate and segment your feedback within the high-level categories such as:
  - Sales performance
    - Your sales performance
    - Sales presentation
    - Sales materials (e.g., proposal/RFP response, presentation handouts)
    - The sales performance of others on your team with whom you sell (if applicable)
    - The sales performance of any intermediaries through which you sell (if applicable)
    - Site visit (if applicable)
  - Product or service issues
    - Strengths and deficiencies in your company's existing suite
    - Product gaps/missing features
    - Technology (if applicable)
  - Client/customer service
  - Price
  - Brand image of your firm
    - Name brand recognition
    - Commitment to your marketplace
    - Perceptions of your company's brand/reputation
- Create a two-page dashboard of all the reasons you win and lose business, complete with percentages from bids won and bids lost prospects and specific reasons/micro-attributes (three to five things that are being articulated by prospects) within each top-level category.
- Aggregate and analyze your postdecision debrief interviews every six months (or at least every year).

Gather Feedback from Your Sales Manager or Sales Mentor

- Meet with your sales manager or sales mentor, and discuss prospects' reasons for winning and losing.
- Ask your sales manager for her opinion of what you are finding and let her offer solutions.

* Approaching your sales manager for this type of advice will help you to build your relationship with her.

Gather Feedback from Colleagues with Whom You Sell

* If you are involved in team selling situations in which you conduct sales presentations with other people in your company (or intermediaries), meet with these people and discuss your prospect feedback.
* Additionally, always debrief with your sales colleagues after each sales meeting. Three key questions that salespeople should ask other presentation team members after a sales presentation:
  1. What three things do you think I (or we) did well?
  2. What three things do you think I (or we) could improve on?
  3. What is the one thing that I (or we) didn't do that you'd like to see me (or us) do?

Gather Input from Top Producing Members of Your Sales Team

* Spend time with the top sales performers of your team. Bounce off of them the insights you've learned from prospects and get their opinions.

PART 3

LEVERAGING WHAT YOU'VE LEARNED

Benchmark Your Feedback

In the final part of this book we will review data from years of research on the sales process, and in the final chapter I will provide you with proven sales techniques based on this research that will help you overcome common sales pitfalls.

In this chapter you will learn five common sales issues that are likely to be impacting your ability to win deals. Based on feedback from thousands of postdecision interviews, a few themes consistently surface regarding why salespeople lose in new business situations. This chapter uses the aggregate results of these interviews to teach you about the most prevalent reasons salespeople lose.

These results come from interviews that have been conducted across a variety of industries; however, one reason for losing in new business situations is universal: sales performance issues. As we outlined in Chapter 2, in an average win/loss analysis program (when conducted by an independent third party), 38 percent of prospects cite sales issues as a deciding factor in a lost deal. Additionally, in 21 percent of bids won situations, prospects also cite sales issues even though they awarded the business to the salesperson.

Several common and negative sales behaviors contribute to these percentages, with the most frequent being a failure on behalf of the salesperson to fully understand and address prospects' unique needs. Figure 7.1 highlights this issue as well as the other most frequently occurring sales concerns, including not making prospects feel

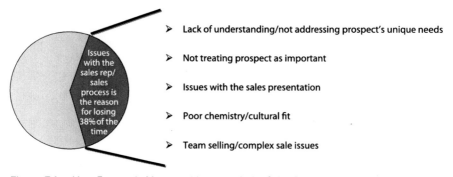

Figure 7.1 Most Frequently Mentioned Issues with the Sales Process

valued, ineffective sales presentations, a lack of chemistry with the prospect/cultural fit with the prospect's organization, and complex sale/team selling issues.

This chapter details each of these five universal pitfalls to enable you to better identify and classify results from your own prospect feedback and, in turn, learn exponentially quicker from your sales mistakes. This will help you benchmark your individual sales performance results from Step 6 to better identify common sales trends within your own prospect feedback cycle. Although individual strengths and weaknesses vary from one salesperson to another, this chapter provides you with a foundational guide to help you get a better sense of what kind of feedback you should be seeking in your postdecision debriefs.

In each section of this chapter, I have also provided actual prospect verbatim quotes so that you can get a better sense of the depth of feedback you should look to receive. At first, these quotes may seem quite critical, but my firm uncovers this type of feedback in roughly 40 percent of sales situations, so don't think that some prospects are not having similar reactions to you. You just haven't heard it before, because you have not been trained to uncover this type of frank criticism. Admittedly, any feedback given to you directly from the prospect may be less cutting than the quotes you will read due to the fact that they were given to an independent third party, but if you use the techniques outlined in Part 2, you too should start to obtain more candid feedback.

Additionally, in many quotes in this chapter, the salesmanship issues that lead to losses, when performed correctly, are key factors in why salespeople win business. When prospects comment negatively about one salesperson's actions, they will often contrast that feedback with positive commentary about the same sales tactic for the winning sales rep. Therefore, as you read each section, recognize that the losing behaviors are also winning behaviors when executed properly.

It is important to note that this chapter focuses exclusively on sales performance and does not include any analysis on product or service issues (e.g., product, pricing, technology, client service, branding, or marketing issues). This does not mean these areas are not important or won't come out as key reasons for why you win and lose, but there are many different industries and product types, so it is impossible to cover them all in this chapter. For the purposes of this book, we are going to focus on the most universal aspect of the sale process: sales performance.

Let's explore five key salesmanship issues in more detail.

UNDERSTANDING AND ADDRESSING THE PROSPECT'S UNIQUE NEEDS

One common sales process shortcoming frequently cited by prospects is that the salesperson failed to understand and address their unique needs/circumstances. This type of feedback manifests itself in several ways, including:

- Salesperson did not perform adequate background research on the prospect/organization
- Salesperson did not ask the right questions
- Salesperson did not listen
- Salesperson was not consultative with the prospect

Performing Adequate Background Research on the Prospect

Prospects frequently mention that the salesperson did not know enough about them or their organizations before they presented their proposed solution. If the salesperson does not know much about the prospect or company, it can be very difficult for the salesperson to make a compelling presentation. It also starts the entire sales process off on the wrong foot and means the prospect must spend time educating the salesperson about things the salesperson should have taken the time to learn on his own.

Following are two examples of real prospect feedback from situations where the salesperson did not perform adequate research before meeting with the prospect. For the purposes of this book, I have scrubbed the actual salesperson and company names and will refer to each salesperson's company as "Sample Company."

The two finalists we selected did more homework than Sample Company. They learned about the culture of our organization, about our people, and about what we did. What these two firms pulled into their presentations distinguished their presentations. For example, we had bios of our people online. They went online and read the bios of the people that would be at the presentation. In one instance, when one presenter introduced himself to one of our people, his comment was, "You look just like in your picture." Another example was the way one firm took what they knew about our people and appealed to what our people were interested in during the presentation. The two finalists had memorized (or at least studied) all of the data out there about our company. They did not spend more time with me but they did their own research. The sales rep and other presentation team members from Sample Company did not do as much research as their counterparts; if they were familiar with our company, it did not show.

The sales rep did not do any background research before she came in. She did not know anything about our business, including the type of company we were, our size, or our product line. She should have known more about us especially since we were already a client on another side of their business.

As you can see, prospects can tell when you have not done your homework. You may think that you can bluff your way through, but there is no substitute for being prepared and learning as much as you can about your audience in advance.

Asking the Right Questions

When prospects mention that salespeople do not understand their unique needs, it is often because salespeople do not ask the right questions (or enough questions) during the sales process. This flaw is perhaps one of the most detrimental sales mistakes that salespeople make. Selling is all about asking questions, and often salespeople (especially those at the beginning of their careers) do not do an adequate job uncovering the needs of prospects or properly qualifying each prospect. The way to overcome this is by asking great questions. Many times, salespeople do not uncover what prospects are truly looking for and have difficulty making great presentations as a result.

> When prospects mention that salespeople do not understand their unique needs, it is often because salespeople do not ask the right questions (or enough questions) during the sales process.

Here is one example of what can happen when a salesperson does not ask all the right questions:

The other competitors we spoke with wanted to go into a lot more detail about our unique needs before meeting with us. They dug very deeply on multiple issues. They uncovered, discovered, and vetted. The prep work they put in was more substantial than Sample Company. In my mind, I appreciate this kind of effort at the front end. There was a pretty big difference between the time I spent with the others going over questions and requirements compared to Sample Company.

When you do a good job of asking great questions and really getting to know prospects, you will impress them with your interest in their situations and businesses. Also, people naturally enjoy talking about themselves, and asking questions gives your prospects a platform and a captive audience. Asking good questions will increase your chances of winning the business, not only because the prospect will like and respect you more, but also because you will be in a much better position to execute throughout the sales process.

Listening

There is an old sales saying that goes, "You've got two ears and one mouth; use them in that proportion." In situations where salespeople spend too much time talking and not enough time listening, they focus most of their value proposition on information that is largely irrelevant to the prospects involved. This issue again comes down to the salesperson's inability to identify the true needs of the prospect in advance of the sales presentation. Many salespeople do not take enough time to listen, and listening is critical in selling.

Here are some examples from salespeople who did not adequately listen to prospects:

The salesperson lost this deal because of the presentation. I gave the sales rep insight into what our company was looking for and coached him before the presentation. He was either too busy, not engaged, did not listen, or did not understand what I said.

Our consultant asked each firm to cover certain topics at the presentation. This was a test to see if a company would listen to us and do what we asked. The sales rep from Sample Company did not listen at all. He went out of his way to sell us in a sales speech. We had already identified his company as a finalist and were past this. We got fluff, no substance. The other two finalists were very responsive to our request. We were able to get a sense of what it would be like working with them. We picked up on which companies delivered what we asked for and which did not. The fact that the sales presentation did not address our specifications made it very clear that Sample Company did not listen to us.

Prospects can tell when salespeople are not listening intently. It often comes across in the salesperson's presentations and interactions with the prospect during the sales process. Even if you ask the right questions, you will still have trouble addressing the prospect's needs if you don't pay attention to the answers.

Being Consultative

A lack of a consultative approach is the final explanation that prospects tend to give for why salespeople do not fully understand their needs. Being consultative involves the previous three aspects we have reviewed. It involves asking great questions, listening attentively, and performing background research on prospects (and companies) so that the salesperson truly collaborates with prospects in developing the right solutions for their organizations.

Here is an example of a situation in which the prospect felt that the salesperson was not being consultative:

We knew they reviewed our situation and understood it at a baseline level. However, we would have liked to see them analyze our current situation and make recommendations on ways to make our business richer, even if they did so just to give us ideas to consider. We liked the winning firm the best because they offered lots of helpful suggestions to streamline and eliminate the manual interventions we had been doing. The winning firm put recommendations in writing for us to consider; they were more consultative.

Being consultative involves the finer points of truly understanding each prospect's unique needs. It involves not only doing research, asking questions, and listening, but then taking the knowledge acquired to the next level. In order to be consultative, you must show that you understand each prospect's situation and make suggestions about how your product or service can meet the needs they are aware of as well as those they may not have even thought of.

As this section shows, salespeople often do not identify what prospects are looking for. As you conduct your debriefs, use your initial decision making criteria questions to identify the factors that were most important to the prospect when selecting the winning vendor. This will allow you to compare the prospect's actual decision drivers with your own perceptions of what was important to them, and, as a result, you will have a better gauge at how successful you are at assessing prospect needs.

> In order to be consultative, you must show that you understand each prospect's situation and make suggestions about how your product or service can meet the needs they are aware of as well as those they may not have even thought of.

> When you don't accurately identify each prospect's unique needs, problems will arise as the sales process progresses.

As you will see in the following sections, when you don't accurately identify each prospect's unique needs, problems will arise as the sales process progresses. An accurate needs assessment is "table stakes" for a successful sales process. It's hard to win if you don't know what the prospect wants.

TREATING PROSPECTS AS VALUED CUSTOMERS

The second most frequently mentioned area where the sales process breaks down may surprise you. Prospects often comment that the salesperson and his company did not demonstrate a strong desire to win their business or assure the prospects that they would be made to feel valued once they became a customer. After aggregating, reviewing, and basing this book on years of actual prospect feedback, this has been one of the most interesting discoveries.

Given the amount of money companies spend on each prospective client during the sales process, it would seem that demonstrating a desire for the business would be inherent, but it is not. In fact, one-third of prospects who cite the sales approach as a key reason for not selecting a company attribute their concern to not feeling important. If the prospects do not feel important to the sales rep, then they will often infer that they will not be important customers to the company.

Sales personnel should make every prospect feel like an important potential client 100 percent of the time. Now, you might argue that not all prospects are good fits for your company, but if you're going to spend the time going after the business, then you need to convey to the prospects that they would be important. Otherwise, don't waste your time or theirs. Prospects often comment that salespeople spend too much time selling them a product versus offering them a solution to a problem. If you're not able to solve a prospect's problem, then accept that it's not a good fit and spend time on prospects whose problems you can address.

There are four salesmanship issues that can make prospects feel unimportant: prospects perceive that they are just another sale for the books; lack of responsiveness from the salesperson; the prospect perceives the salesperson to be arrogant; and the

> **One-third of prospects who cite the sales approach as a key reason for not selecting a company attribute their concern to not feeling important.**

salesperson's company's size makes prospects feel like they would be "a small fish in a big pond."

Let's explore each of these issues in more detail.

Just Another Sale for the Books

One major way in which prospects cite that they feel unimportant to salespeople is when they perceive that the salesperson is only in it for the commission check. Prospects often feel that salespeople are not genuine in their efforts and, therefore, it makes prospects feel insignificant. They feel that the salesperson is only in it to close the deal and doesn't really care about the long term needs of the prospect.

Following is a quote from a prospect who did not feel important during the sales process:

> *Throughout the sales process, I had a feeling that my business was being approached strictly as a sales call . . . a deal to close for the books. I did not feel comfortable that the sales rep was invested in the long haul with me, and this is an impression of how it might have been with the company as a whole. The rep was very, very knowledgeable and knew the product in and out, but I could not get comfortable that the company was going to deliver the service and long term relationship that means a lot to me. I decided to stay where I've been. The big negative was the overall tone or feeling of the sales process. My impression was that it was a sales operation first, not a service opportunity. I felt like they were looking for the win and then they would forget about us.*

Remember, the prospect's perception is reality, so even if you feel that you always treat prospects as important, some may perceive the opposite.

Responsiveness

Poor responsiveness is a selling blunder that is entirely within the control of the salesperson. While this is not a major issue among most salespeople, it does come up, and when it does, it makes prospects feel like the salesperson does not want their business. As a salesperson, you are often the initial first impression that a customer or prospect will have of your company. When a salesperson is not responsive to prospects, prospects infer that the salesperson's company will not be responsive to them once they become customers. Therefore, they will feel unimportant.

> When a salesperson is not responsive to prospects, prospects infer that the salesperson's company will not be responsive to them once they become customers.

Here are some quotes that exemplify this type of sales issue:

It took months for the sales rep to get back to me. When he finally did and we set up a time to meet, he came down here and approached the meeting with the assumption that his company was automatically going to be selected. He basically demoed the product and said, "Sign on the line." I asked for some additional information and was told it would be sent to me. I never heard back. Weeks went by and still nothing. He dropped the ball.

The sales rep traveled a lot and was in conferences often so was difficult to reach. We had to exchange a lot of voice mails. Sometimes he did not provide me with everything I asked for or gave me the wrong information. His responses were not timely enough.

In all my years of research, one thing I have never heard is a prospect state that he felt the salesperson was too responsive or too quick to get back to him to resolve issues or answer questions. Being responsive can be one of your greatest competitive differentiators as a salesperson. Being responsive not only shows prospects that you care about them and makes them feel important,

> Being responsive can be one of your greatest competitive differentiators as a salesperson.

but it also differentiates you from all the other salespeople who take days to get back to prospects for simple answers to their questions.

Arrogance

Perceived arrogance is another issue that ends some sales processes as soon as they begin. When a salesperson comes off as all-knowing or condescending to a prospect, this can be a challenging situation and often makes prospects feel unimportant. It is one thing to be confident; it is another to be arrogant.

Additionally, the root cause of a perception of arrogance can come from other places, such as your company's position in the marketplace. For example, if you sell for a market leader, some prospects will have a preconceived notion about you and your company before entering into a sales cycle. Here is a sample quote from a prospect who perceived a sales rep as arrogant due to her company's positioning in the marketplace:

> *They came in with an attitude that came across as they were all-knowing; because they were an industry leader, they did not have to prove themselves. They had an arrogance about them. They should have sold us on their customer service instead of resting on their laurels. We did not like their attitude at the presentation and were concerned about what they would be like to work with . . . In the end, they came in third. They did not try to prove themselves to us, and they failed to win the account because of it. No effort was made to customize the presentation . . . The winning firm did a great job making us feel confident they could do the job and that they wanted the account.*

No one likes to be called arrogant, and salespeople are always shocked when they receive feedback that a prospect viewed them this way. Remember, some of what you do may be perceived the wrong way. Even if you didn't mean to come off that way, you may have to alter how you approach each sales situation.

As a further example, I will share with you a personal lesson I learned when I was an inexperienced salesperson early in my career. I was preparing to make a presentation to an important prospect/

committee. Since I was inexperienced, when I spoke with my prospect (who was in a very senior role at his company) over the phone to set up the sales presentation and he asked me how much time I would need, I told him that I could do it in 45 minutes if need be. I immediately assumed that since the prospect was so senior in the organization, he would not want me to take up much of his time. However, an interesting thing happened that changed the way I thought about selling. The prospect actually knew my sales manager quite well and told him, "If Rich didn't feel that the presentation was important enough to spend more time with me, we can cancel the whole thing."

My sales manager and I were shocked when we heard this news. Neither of us could understand how I would have given anyone the impression that they were not important or that I could come across as arrogant in this situation. However, I quickly realized that my own inexperience was at fault for making the prospect feel unimportant. It was a great lesson for me that simple miscommunications by salespeople can easily and unintentionally cause prospects to feel unimportant.

A Small Fish in a Big Pond

Sometimes the sheer size of your company will make prospects feel like they will become "another number" or "small fish in a big pond." This happens quite often in sales situations for big companies. If you sell for a big company with many customers, prospects might fear feeling insignificant, and you will need to address this with them on a proactive basis.

> Sometimes the sheer size of your company will make prospects feel like they will become "another number" or "small fish in a big pond."

Here is a quote in which a prospect felt he would not be an important client because of how many customers the selling firm had:

They are a large company. Based on our experience, being a small fish in a big pond likely means that the service is not as good as it would be from a smaller company. We did not think we were a big enough deal for this large company.

Treating prospects as though they would be important customers is critical in winning deals. There are a variety of ways in which prospects perceive that salespeople make them feel unimportant. As you begin to get your own feedback from prospects, try to home in on whether or not you are making each prospect feel valued. Similar to the challenges of not correctly identifying each prospect's needs, when prospects don't feel important, it will cause you problems in all areas of the sales process.

ISSUES WITH THE SALES PRESENTATION

Presentations are another area in which prospects cite multiple issues. Most people assume that when presentations go poorly, the salesperson should be aware of it. However, at times this is not the case. Subtle things can go wrong in a presentation that the salesperson may not see, and unless they are pointed out, the salesperson and company run the risk of repeating the same mistakes again and again.

There are four main areas that prospects cite with respect to how sales presentations could have been improved: lack of preparedness; lack of customization to the presentation to show that the salesperson understood the prospect's unique needs; lack of salesperson's product or industry knowledge; and lack of differentiation.

Win/loss research reveals that despite where a company ranks among competitors going into the final sales presentation, a poor presentation will leave the prospect with an unsettling impression and often results in a lost sale.

Preparedness

Preparation is one of the most important aspects of the sales process. It results in strong execution and also leads to confidence and enthusiasm—all critical ingredients to a successful sales presentation.

You simply must strive to "own" your sales presentations, because if you don't, your competitors will, and they will win the business.

The following prospect quotes illustrate how lack of preparation influences the sales outcome:

Sample Company was less prepared than the other two finalists. They were not ill prepared; I do not want to fault the sales rep. They tackled all they needed to, but the other two sales reps overprepared. They left no stone unturned. This was a fairly complex sales situation, so the client hired me as an independent consultant to help them find the best solution. The other two finalists wanted to go into a lot more detail with me about the finer points of the deal before meeting with the client. They both dug very deeply on multiple issues.

We were not as impressed by Sample Company's presentation or the people involved. Their sales team was not organized and lacked the right people. We could tell that the winning firm had practiced the presentation many times. The winning firm included key people who were prepared and impressive.

As these quotes suggest, it can also be the case where your competitors simply prepare more than you. It may not be that you're unprepared but that the competition does more prep work to impress the prospect and outsell you to win the deal.

Customization

Another critical sales presentation issue involves a lack of customization to each prospect's particular situation. Prospects frequently feel that sales presentations are "canned" and not tailored to their unique needs. This is often a byproduct of the issues we explored earlier in this chapter regarding understanding the prospect's unique needs. Additionally, if a prospect feels that you did not customize your message, it will be hard for her to feel important.

> Prospects frequently feel that sales presentations are "canned" and not tailored to their unique needs.

Here is a quote from a prospect who felt that an RFP response was not customized:

I think the RFP response could have been more tailored to our company. The other vendors really customized their responses. The competition went out of their way to show that they had clients in our field. Sample Company did not tailor their response at all . . . I think the other players are better at customizing their capabilities and RFP responses. Sample Company will need to do a better job of responding to RFPs if they want to get into these types of deal situations in the future.

Customizing your presentation does not necessarily mean that you need to recreate all your sales materials. Customization comes as much from what you say as it does from what you show the prospect.

Product/Industry Knowledge

Another sales presentation comment commonly referenced by prospects is that the salesperson was not knowledgeable about their product or industry. This can be problematic because often prospects need to be educated by salespeople about the specifics of how a product or service works. When a salesperson comes across as unknowledgeable, prospects will likely lose confidence and choose a firm with a salesperson who better understands their particular product or industry.

Following are some examples of prospects who viewed their salesperson as unknowledgeable.

My sales rep was totally uneducated about the product. At the core level, I needed to know what the product could and could not do. It was totally confusing because he did not understand the product at all. This stream of bad information wasted three weeks of my time and research.

Although the sales rep would get high marks from me in regard to the sales presentation and his sales skills, the fact was that his product knowledge was low. I do not know why the sales rep was not aware of the product's integration capabilities (or lack thereof). I feel like I was incorrectly sold a bill of goods and that the sales rep was uninformed about the product.

Limited product or industry knowledge can severely limit a salesperson's ability to make a great presentation. You can be the best presenter in the world, but if you don't understand your product, you will lack substance. And if you aren't knowledgeable about your industry, you will not be able to speak proficiently about your competition. If you lack knowledge, it will be hard for you to instill confidence in your audience or to transfer enthusiasm to them about what you are selling. All else being equal, prospects want to buy from experts.

> Limited product or industry knowledge can severely limit a salesperson's ability to make a great presentation. You can be the best presenter in the world, but if you don't understand your product, you will lack substance.

Differentiation

Another recurring sales presentation issue involves salespeople's ability to differentiate themselves, their companies, and their products and services from the competition. Differentiating one's pitch is perhaps the highest art form of making a great presentation. Making your sales presentations distinctive not only involves strong execution of the fundamentals, but it also involves delivering some form of creativity within your pitch. In order to differentiate yourself, you really must know your product well, and you must be able to articulate how you are different from your competition. This can be very difficult, especially in industries where the product or service is largely commoditized.

Here are some quotes about salespeople who struggled to differentiate their pitches during the sales process:

They came across as competent, knowledgeable, and friendly, but they didn't differentiate themselves. At no point did they come out and say, "Here is where we are better." They seemed to know us but didn't use that knowledge to take the presentation to the next level.

We were not closed-minded about changing vendors. However, if Sample Company wanted to win, they had to do a better job differentiating themselves. We did not see a compelling reason to switch. Their pricing and technology were similar to what we currently had. Sample Company needs to show what makes them different. Otherwise, they are just going to be a commodity item.

Articulating how you are different is an advanced part of selling. You need to not only understand yourself and your company but also the competitive landscape of your industry. You will need to understand your competition, because it will be impossible to articulate how you are different if you don't know anything about them. This

> **Differentiating one's pitch is perhaps the highest art form of making a great presentation.**

is why newer salespeople often have a harder time differentiating themselves against more mature sales professionals. Differentiation comes with experience, seasoning, and a commitment to your profession.

When you are debriefing with prospects, you should always probe how your sales presentations can be improved. Many of the questions suggested in Chapter 4 can be used to uncover this type of valuable feedback. Even if your sales presentation is not the primary reason you lost, often prospects will share valuable insights that will help you to refine your presentations in the future.

CHEMISTRY/CULTURAL FIT WITH ORGANIZATION

The fourth area where prospects often mention a disconnect during the sales process is with respect to the personal chemistry they feel with the salesperson or with the salesperson's organization. Many salespeople feel there isn't much they can do about their ability to have chemistry with prospects, which is not altogether false—as you know, you click with some people better than others. It is a fact, however, that the very best salespeople are the ones who can get along with the most people. While chemistry cannot always be overcome, there are several tactics one can take to improve the likelihood of connecting with a prospect, such as preparation and planning. We will further explore these techniques in Chapter 8.

There are three main issues that prospects cite when they give feedback with respect to a lack of chemistry with salespeople: inability to build rapport, regional/cultural differences, and salespeople coming across as overly aggressive or pushy. Let's review each of these areas in more detail.

Building Rapport

The ability to develop a sense of chemistry with prospects comes early on in the sales process. When a prospect does not feel chemistry with the salesperson, it is usually because the salesperson could have done a better job at taking more time to build rapport at the beginning of the sales cycle versus rushing into "the hard sell." Many times, salespeople do not spend enough time getting to know prospects on a more personal level before moving on into the sales process.

The sales process has a flow to it, and just as you should identify what the prospect is looking for before you make a sales presentation, you should also establish some type of rapport before you identify prospect needs. Building rapport and developing chemistry with prospects is one of the more difficult aspects of the sales process, not only because some elements of personal chemistry are outside your control, but also because there is often significant time pressure put on salespeople (especially at the beginning of a sales cycle). Additionally, each prospect is different. Some like to take time at the beginning of a sales process to get to know you, and others like to get right into the sales discussion. Some prospect situations will seem effortless in your ability to develop rapport, and others will seem very difficult.

> Building rapport and developing chemistry with prospects is one of the more difficult aspects of the sales process, not only because some elements of personal chemistry are outside your control, but also because there is often significant time pressure put on salespeople (especially at the beginning of a sales cycle).

Here is a prospect quote that illustrates the need for rapport building:

There was a concern on our part that we did not connect with the salesperson immediately. It may have been that he was quiet, but we did not think he was as strong as the other salespeople. Again, it could have been his personality, the lack of rapport between us, or his understanding of the business. All of us on the committee felt this way. The salespeople we met from the other firms were easy for us to build a rapport with. We felt they would be honest with us and straightforward.

The best antidote to a lack of chemistry with prospects is preparation. As mentioned earlier, prospects can tell when you are prepared, and this will put them at ease at the beginning of a sales conversation. Additionally, the more you prepare, the more flexible you can be with how you approach each prospect. There-

> **The best antidote to a lack of chemistry with prospects is preparation.**

fore, depending on how much rapport you feel with a prospect at the beginning of a sales cycle, you will be able to alter your approach and presentation style to best fit the needs of the prospect.

Regional/Cultural Differences

In addition to the personal chemistry that may or may not occur between the prospect and the salesperson, cultural chemistry between the prospect and salesperson's organizations is important to the sales process. Often, the end decision comes down to how well the prospect "likes" the selling company and its employees and/or if there is a cultural fit between the two companies. While a salesperson can adjust his strategy to prevail over a lack of rapport between individuals, a organization-wide mismatch in chemistry and cultural fit is more difficult to overcome. For example, it may be that the prospect's company is small and is in an industry where relationships are of the utmost importance to their business. If the prospect is looking at a very large, technology-focused company where the relationship is formed primarily via the Internet, there may be a disconnect. In this scenario, the prospect may connect with the people he meets during the sales process, but if he knows that his personal, one-on-one contact will be limited, he may decide there is not a good "fit."

> *Part of our decision was based on how we fit by industry, demographics, and corporate culture into the entity chosen. Sample Company was the most progressive of the companies we looked at. We are a stodgy manufacturing company, and Sample Company was too progressive. They were too technologically based for our company and culture. The firm we selected relied less on technology and more on people. They had a higher-touch service model that worked better for our culture.*

> The definition of "pushy" varies from prospect to prospect, so it is important to feel out the prospect and establish a cadence of communication that is mutually acceptable early on in the sales process.

Being Too Pushy or Overly Aggressive

Another common sales flaw that is often seen in less experienced sales organizations is aggressive behavior or pushiness. The definition of "pushy" varies from prospect to prospect, so it is important to feel out the prospect and establish a cadence of communication that is mutually acceptable early on in the sales process. It is one thing to be persistent, but being pushy means that you are following up too much and not understanding how the prospect wants to progress during the sales process.

Following are some quotes that exemplify this situation:

> *We had significant issues with the sales rep. I would describe her as "very pushy." I'm sure in this business she has to be that way to a certain extent, but my advice would be for her to pull it back a little. She also talks a lot and doesn't listen so well. Even after we told her that her company had lost, we were still getting phone calls from her, which we equated to whining.*

> *They called me too much. Follow-up is good, and I appreciate it, but someone needs to tell their sales team about balance. There is a good bal-*

ance between too little follow-up and too much. I got calls every day from Sample Company . . . too much!

When debriefing with prospects, sometimes the best way to assess your personal chemistry with them is by listening to how they speak about the other salesperson(s) and/or about the winning firm's culture. The competitive assessment questions in Chapter 4 are great places to uncover areas where your ability to build rapport can be improved.

COMPLEX SALE/TEAM SELLING ISSUES

The final area of salesmanship issues involves team selling situations. Team selling happens frequently in large deal situations in which prospects meet the team with which they will be working on a day-to-day basis once the sales process is over. Or, if it is a more technical sale, prospects may need to meet with technology personnel in order to better understand what they are being sold and how it will fit their needs.

> **Whenever you expand the number of people presenting to a prospect, you increase your level of exposure to potential salesmanship issues.**

Whenever you expand the number of people presenting to a prospect, you increase your level of exposure to potential salesmanship issues. That said, it is obviously imperative to the sales process that the prospect meet the appropriate contacts, and the prospect will be more likely to feel valued if you take the time to introduce everyone. Therefore, it is critical that all members of the sales team work together and get feedback on their performance so that everyone can understand how important his or her individual role is in securing new business.

There are three key areas that prospects mention in complex/team selling new business situations: lack of key personnel/mix of personnel at the presentation; issues with individual sales presentation team members/weaker presenters; and lack of cohesiveness. Let's review each of these areas in more detail.

Mix of Personnel at the Presentation

One significant issue that can arise during team selling situations is when the mix of sales presentation team members is not what the prospect was expecting. This can happen because either there are missing presentation team members or because the mix of personnel is not well balanced. In complex sales situations, prospects often want to meet the team of people with whom they would be working, and, as the below quotes show, if this team is not present or does not present well, it can often result in a lost sale.

> *Although I really feel that she did a good job as a sales rep, we ultimately agreed that the winning firm's team was a lot more energetic and, as a result, they connected better with us. Sample Company's sales team was much more serious than the winning team, and it came across as a little stodgy . . . Also, we never met anyone from their client service area, whereas the winning firm brought in our actual client service people during the presentation. It was good to be able to look the person in the eye and get a feel for what it would be like to work with him.*

Additionally, issues with the mix of personnel can also be the result of diversity issues, not just the mix between sales, marketing, technology, and service personnel.

> *We are a nonprofit organization that assists women in a variety of areas. Furthermore, the committee that made this decision was [composed] primarily of women. Sample Company's presentation team did not have any women on it. In contrast, the winning firm sent in a team of women, including the president of the company, who was female. Sample Company may want to consider the composition of the audience when putting a team together. They also should have put together material that was better suited for the female demographics of our workforce.*

It is critical to bring the right people to each presentation. Whether these are technical or service people or whether you have the right gender or diversity mix, prospects often notice when a sales team does not have the right blend of personnel.

Less Experienced Presenters

Another important issue that negatively impacts prospect perceptions is when weaker sales presentation team members present during a team sales approach. Prospects frequently comment on less experienced members of the sales presentation team or when client service personnel are brought in to meet with prospects. These businesspeople are typically not accustomed to making sales presentations, and they often come across as unprepared or inexperienced. The following quotes will help you get a feel for how prospects perceive these types of personnel.

The client service rep did not come across well during the presentation. He lacked confidence. He was somber and not outgoing enough. He did not take command of the room or the client. The client did not feel he would manage the relationship well. The client service rep needed to present and communicate better. The winning firm spent most of their time talking about the quality of their people and were able to show the client service rep in the best possible way.

The one problem we had with the presentation team was with the client service representative. He was experienced but was not the type of individual we wanted working with us in difficult situations. We were not sure how he would handle them. When you only have a short time to shape your impression of an individual and that impression is not strong, it can take you a long time to get over it. We did not want to take any risks. If this individual is going to be put in front of potential clients, he has to be able to establish a rapport with the people in the room and make a positive impression on them. This did not happen . . . He was not someone we wanted to work with. We had concerns about him being able to navigate us through issues or tough situations. He was the one reason they lost the business.

Additionally, a lack of presentation abilities can end up leaving the prospect with the impression that other presentation team members are not excited to be at the meeting, and therefore, prospects can feel unimportant.

We got the impression from the individual that would be our day-to-day contact that it was not important to him that Sample Company win this account. He did not jump through any hoops for us. He was not warm and fuzzy toward us, and this turned us off. He may have been a good accountant, but that is not all that counts.

Although these types of issues can be frustrating for sales personnel, it is ultimately your responsibility to quarterback the selling team. Whether you choose to address this issue through training or enhanced preparation, candid prospect feedback shared with these less experienced team members can be a powerful catalyst for change and development.

Cohesiveness

Each of the preceding team selling issues can leave the prospect feeling that there was a lack of cohesiveness during the presentation. Lack of cohesiveness can be symptomatic of multiple issues, including lack of preparation, contrasting presentation styles and personalities, egos, and a mix of experienced and less experienced or nervous presenters.

As the following quotes show, lack of cohesiveness is a much cited comment by prospects during team sale debriefs.

The presentation team as a whole did not work well together. For example, one team member interjected a comment during another team member's presentation that contradicted what the team member was saying. This was not a cohesive group; it was clear they had not worked together a lot before. The presentation was not choreographed well.

The sales rep could have done more to prepare the team for the presentation. He should have gone over it with the team beforehand. He also could have worked in the other sales team members better. There were conflicting stories told by individuals on the team. They should have prepared a cohesive story . . . The sales presentation lacked a prepared, customized approach. It looked like it had been pulled together last minute.

Cohesiveness is critical during team selling presentations, and when a team does not come across as a cohesive unit, it is typically a signal of a lack of preparation. It is only through dry runs and consistent preparation

> **When a team does not come across as a cohesive unit, it is typically a signal of a lack of preparation.**

that the best selling teams become successful. Just as being consultative is the highest form of understanding prospects' unique needs and differentiating yourself is the top distinction for making a great presentation, cohesiveness is the highest compliment a selling team can receive.

CHAPTER WRAP-UP

There are many different things that can go wrong during the sales process. By reviewing each of these areas in more detail, you should now understand the types of salesmanship "red flags" that you should look out for as you debrief with prospects. By implementing the tactics in this book, you will be able to garner more of the type of feedback you read in this chapter. This feedback may be painful at first, but over time you will become stronger as you begin to act on the feedback and compensate for these issues. If you haven't heard this type of candor from your prospects, you have not been getting the true reasons you win and lose.

In the final chapter of this book, I will show you how to take action on your feedback, and you will learn time-tested sales techniques that will help you overcome many of the commonly cited sales issues we have explored in this chapter.

CHAPTER SUMMARY

The Five Most Common Reasons Salespeople Lose Deals

* Lack of understanding and addressing prospects' unique needs.
  * Salesperson did not perform sufficient background research on the prospect/organization.
  * Salesperson did not ask the right questions.
  * Salesperson did not listen.
  * Salesperson was not consultative with prospect.
* Not treating prospects as if they would be valued customers.
  * Prospects perceive that they are just another sale.
  * Lack of responsiveness.
  * Arrogance.
  * Your company's size makes prospects feel like small fish in a big pond.
* Issue with the sales presentation.
  * Lack of preparedness.
  * Lack of customization to the presentation to show that the salesperson understood the prospect's unique needs.
  * Lack of salesperson's product or industry knowledge.
  * Lack of differentiation.
* Lack of personal chemistry or cultural fit with prospect/the prospect's organization.
  * Inability to build rapport.
  * Regional/cultural differences.
  * Salesperson comes across as pushy/aggressive.
* Complex sale/team selling issues.
  * Lack of key personnel/mix of personnel at the presentation.
  * Issues with individual sales presentation team members/weaker presenters.
  * Lack of cohesiveness.

STEP 8

Implement the Right Techniques to Increase Your Close Rate

This final chapter provides actionable advice on how to successfully address the common sales process stumbling blocks identified in Chapter 7, allowing you a jump start on identifying and acting on your own personal areas for improvement. This sales execution advice has been developed with thousands of salespeople and institutional clients over the last decade. These sales techniques have been tested and proven over and over again, and they are applicable in almost any sales situation. There are many books on the market that will give you advice on selling, but this tactical sales advice will help you during the sales process as well as during the debrief process.

I have purposely saved the sales training for the last chapter. If you have taken the advice in the previous chapters and begun to implement a program for gathering more accurate and comprehensive prospect feedback, you will be in a much better position to understand what you need to do to improve your salesmanship.

As I mentioned earlier in the book, most salespeople forget what they learn at sales training seminars 48 hours after they are done. I did not cite this because I think sales training is not valuable—in fact, I think sales training is incredibly valuable and can be quite motivating. However, sales training is much more effective if you approach it having first discovered your own individual strengths and weaknesses. Once your areas for improvement have been diag-

> **Sales training is much more effective if you approach it having first discovered your own individual strengths and weaknesses.**

nosed, you are better positioned to learn from sales training and implement solutions.

This final chapter will leave you with ideas and sales tactics that apply to any salesperson across all industries. These nuggets of information have been distilled from the thousands of interviews my firm has conducted, and they are timeless principles of sales execution that can help you win more business.

TRACK YOUR CLOSE RATE

The first piece of sales advice I would give anyone who wants to win more business is to calculate and track your close rate. The very first step in improving anything is to determine a variable to measure your performance and set a baseline target. If you don't know your close rate, it will be impossible for you to ever tell if you are improving. True, many of you can tell what kind of year you've had compared with the prior by using other metrics, such as revenue produced or number of deals sold, but I want you to also begin tracking your close rate. Close rate is the best proxy for your true day-in, day-out sales effectiveness. To use a baseball analogy, your close rate would equate to your batting average. You could have a good year in terms of revenue by landing one or two monster deals (home runs), but your close rate (batting average) might still be low.

Do you know your personal close rate? Have you ever paused from your daily routine to come up with a percentage of how often you win and lose in new business situations? It is surprising how few salespeople actually know their exact close rates.

If you have not made an accurate assessment of your close rate, here's how to do it. First look back on all the deals you have bid on over the last 12 months. At first, include only real deal situations in which you have made an actual sales presentation in person. Do not include situations in which you or your company did not actually *meet* with a prospect. Now that you have the number of real deals you have bid on, calculate the number of wins and then divide that number by the number of total deals. Let's say you make 50 sales presentations per year and you win 15 of them. In this scenario, you would have a 30 percent win rate (15/50 = 30 percent). Also, depending on what business you are in and the length of your sales process, you may want to extend the time period you track. For example, consider tracking your win rate over a two-year period.

Two other ways to calculate your close rate include:

1. *Win rate by company.* This is your ability to turn a company into a customer or client.
2. *Win rate by proposal.* This is a more refined metric in which you take the percentage of wins among prospects or existing clients for whom you have written formal proposals.

There are a number of other useful sales metrics you may wish to track. For example, you could track the number of cold calls you make that turn into sales meetings. You could also track your win rate by when you meet with decision makers versus key influencers to identify if you are more successful selling when you get in front of decision makers (as opposed to people who are simply influencing the outcome). However, for the purposes of this book and program, the most relevant metrics are win rate by company and win rate by proposal, as this book is about how to make your sales meetings and presentations better, not about how to enhance your cold calling capabilities.

Since the primary metric this book is intended to help you improve is your close rate, a key first step is to set a baseline by figuring out your current close rate. If you are not keeping score, you will be less inclined to pay attention to what you need to do to increase your score. I often use the analogy of a basketball game to make this point. Have you ever noticed that when you watch a pickup basketball game and the players are not keeping score, they tend to play with less intensity? However, once the players decide to keep score, all of a sudden everyone starts playing harder, and people will start diving for the ball and sweating more. This is no different in business. If you don't keep score, you won't play as hard. Even if you are keeping track of your commissions, it is your new business win rate that is ultimately driving your paycheck. By determining an accurate ratio of how often you win in new business situations, you will find yourself thinking and working on your sales effectiveness more and more.

Some of you may be thinking that tracking your commission and compensation is keeping score, and I do agree with you to some extent. However, we all know that commission plans change from year to year and can work in your favor or against you. Additionally, one big deal could make your whole year and skew your results either positively or negatively; therefore, the truest and most pure way to track your sales effectiveness is by looking at your close rate. Your close rate is never compromised by changing compensation plans or by one lucky (or unlucky) deal.

START AT THE TOP: SELL TO THE DECISION MAKER

Think back to all your sales situations over the last year. How many meetings did you have with real decision makers versus day-to-day, champion-type prospects? If you are having too many meetings with people who aren't real decision makers, you need to rethink your sales strategy. You need to focus on getting more meetings with the right people.

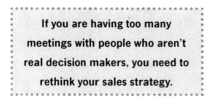

If you are having too many meetings with people who aren't real decision makers, you need to rethink your sales strategy.

You don't need more meetings; you just need better meetings with actual buyers.

I often see this as a problem in big companies where salespeople are expected to schedule a target number of sales meetings per week. This type of sales activity log requirement often leads to a lot of "subpar" meetings that can't really be classified as "true" sales meetings because the decision makers are not involved.

Instead of spending time writing proposals for people who aren't in a position to hire you or buy your product, the goal of these meetings should be to gain access to end decision makers. Just say at the end of the meeting, "Well, Mr. Prospect, thank you for meeting with me today. The information you provided is incredibly valuable. It appears that this decision will be made by Ms. X, would you mind if I follow up with her?" Or ask the person you are meeting with to sponsor a meeting with the decision maker.

Once you have identified the true decision maker, don't let the prospect talk you out of calling on that individual. An excuse I commonly hear an influencer prospect offer is, "I wouldn't call on her because she is so busy you'll probably never get a meeting. Instead I would start with Mr. Y." What this person is actually saying is, "Why don't I put you in a holding pattern and send you to yet another gatekeeper?" When you hear this type of stalling, it means the person you are speaking with may lack political capital within the organization, or he may feel you lack the appropriate seniority to meet with his boss, or you simply may not have impressed him enough to merit his brokering a meeting with the decision maker. Entering into a company at too low a level can put you in a bind—if you get stuck at the wrong level, it is challenging to get out because it is politically risky to go over your contact's head.

I often use the analogy of a plane ride to make this point. When you are flying in a plane at lower altitudes, the air is choppier and the plane tends to hit more turbulence. When the plane increases its altitude, the ride is smoother and you hit fewer bumps. This is a great analogy to selling at the top. When you sell at the top, you will have fewer bumps and your ride will be smoother.

Here are some of the benefits of selling to top executives:

- *You'll have less to do after each sales meeting.* When you focus all of your sales calls on the right decision maker, you will have fewer follow-up requests and meetings. When you meet with someone who is not the decision maker, you typically have to set up subsequent meetings with those who are actually responsible for making the decisions. This can be very time consuming, and if you are traveling, it can also become costly.
- *You will have less emotional involvement in each deal.* You will feel better about each situation because you will not need to wonder or worry about whether your champion is actually helping you or hurting you. When you meet with the right person, you can simply wait for her decision and feel good about the fact that you have done all you can do. You also won't

need to spend any time coaching your champion prospect about what to say or how to position your product and service to others in her company (another time-consuming and risky endeavor in which you cede control of the sale).

- *You will get quicker decisions.* The higher up in any organization you go, the more you will find that people make quicker decisions. In many cases, an executive's advancement in a company can be measured by how many decisions that individual makes in a given day. This is not only because it is the executive's job to make decisions but also because decisive people tend to rise to the top of companies. Often, decision making is concentrated among a few people at the top

> Often, decision making is concentrated among a few people at the top of an organization. If you find them, you will have a quicker sales process (as decisions are made much faster).

of an organization. If you find them, you will have a quicker sales process (as decisions are made much faster), and you will be able to move on to the next deal faster. When you meet with more decision makers (and fewer nondecision makers), you will obtain answers much faster and free up the time and emotional headspace to go after more business.

- *You will garner more candid and accurate information on why you win and lose.* When dealing with true decision makers, you will obtain more candid information when you lose because it will not be watered down by various levels of bureaucracy. For example, the reason you lose will not be because your contact was afraid to bring the initiative to his boss or because of internal politics. I have often found that the people at the top of organizations are the best communicators and are more up front with feedback—key skills for executives. Many have sales backgrounds themselves. Therefore, they appreciate your position and respect what you are trying to do. When you get feedback from someone who has an in-depth understanding of sales, you will often get an insightful perspective on why you win and lose (or about what you need to do in order to win the deal).

Decision makers tend to have a broader strategic view of their companies, which puts them in the best position to assess the true value of your products or services. Middle managers are often solely focused on their individual fiefdoms, which can lead to a shortsighted emphasis on price that can be difficult to overcome.

> **When dealing with true decision makers, you will obtain more candid information when you lose because it will not be watered down by various levels of bureaucracy.**

I have personally learned this lesson the hard way through years of selling. In the earlier years of my sales career, I would often take meetings with influencers who were not the main people driving decisions. I viewed these meetings as warm-ups for meetings with the real decision makers, but I learned this strategy did not often pan out. Often, the original person with whom I met would "run with the ball" and try to sell my services internally for me. I was frequently unable to stop this from happening. Once you open up a dialogue with someone who is not the end decision maker, your options become more limited.

For example, your prospect may decide to act as a gatekeeper because she is uncomfortable with you going over her head by meeting with the true decision maker, who may be her boss (or her boss's boss). Or she may like your product/service so much that she wants to take ownership of the idea and champion the initiative. If your prospect is in a politically tenuous situation at work, she may choose not to bring up any new initiatives for fear of repercussions. In any of these situations, your options become increasingly limited, and it becomes difficult for you to maneuver through a company to pitch the right people. Whatever you may gain in information and intelligence in the initial meeting is offset by your inability to get in front of the right people.

In situations where you never meet the decision maker, you will often find that you lose the deal to "no decision," whereby your prospect will tell you "It's just not the right timing," or "We've got a lot of other things on our plate right now." So you will have to follow up in six months or at some later date. These situations cost you valuable time and money and leave you more vulnerable to competitors entering into your target company while you are forced to wait it out on the sidelines.

If you find yourself in a situation where your prospect has pushed off the decision, you should let the time pass and approach the actual decision maker the next time around. Alternatively, you could immediately go over the head of your champion prospect and reach out to the decision maker directly, but you are likely to cause hard feelings and lose your champion as an advocate.

Salespeople frequently complain that their prospects are hiding something from them because they sense that the prospects are not the true decision makers. In fact, 35 percent of salespeople feel that prospects do not give them the candid truth when they lose because the prospects do not want to look bad. However, the salesperson is as much to blame for this type of situation as the prospect. Identifying and targeting the true decision maker is the responsibility of the salesperson. Simple tactics like asking your prospect, "How will this decision be made?" or "Who are the key decision makers?" can help you better identify who you should actually be in front of. Getting to the right person will speed up your sales process and increase your close rate. It will also help you get more accurate information about why you win and lose in new business situations and is perhaps the best antidote for overcoming many of the issues we covered in Part 1.

PREPARE, PREPARE, PREPARE!

Preparation is perhaps the most critical part of being a salesperson. Much of what determines whether you win or lose a deal happens before you even get inside the prospect's office, and everything you do before you interact with the prospect is called preparation. Training for salesmanship is very similar to training for a marathon. You can always tell how much you trained by the time it takes to finish the race. True, there will be some people who are more gifted than others, in both athletics as well as sales. There might be members on your team who are

> Much of what determines whether you win or lose a deal happens before you even get inside the prospect's office, and everything you do before you interact with the prospect is called preparation.

naturally gifted and just know how to win. But the vast majority of salespeople have to work hard at it every day.

The reason preparation is so important is because properly preparing for a sales meeting will make you more impactful in all the other phases of the sales process. Let's review:

- *Getting in the door.* The more prepared you are before making a prospecting call, the more likely you are to get a meeting. For instance, the more you know about a company or prospect, the more likely you'll be able to begin a productive dialogue.
- *Establishing a connection.* The more you prepare before your first interaction with a prospect, the better you will be at building rapport. You will feel more confident in your initial interactions. When you are well prepared, you will exude confidence and enthusiasm because you will be excited to show the prospect how much you've prepared and how valuable your product or service is.
- *Conducting a needs analysis.* The more you prepare before a sales meeting, the better you will be at identifying a prospect's needs. For example, if you develop a great list of sales questions and plan out how each part of the meeting will go, you will be much better able to extract information about what the prospect is really looking for.
- *Presenting.* The area of the sales process that gets the most benefit from preparation is presenting solutions. If you do not prepare well and really plan out what you are going to show the prospect, it will be impossible to give a strong presentation. Preparation also helps you in one very critical area: customization. This is a word frequently used by prospects when giving feedback on salespeople. Everyone wants to feel important and understood, and when you prepare and develop a presentation that comes across as customized, you will be well on your way to winning the business.
- *Answering questions/handling objections.* When you are well prepared, you will also be better at overcoming objections. In fact, one great way to prepare is to come up with a list of what you think the prospect's top five objections might be and what

you will say to overcome them. It is impressive to prospects when you have anticipated their concerns and are able to put them at ease with your answers. This again will help you exude confidence and enthusiasm.

* *Closing the sale.* The more you prepare, the more you will close. Additionally, when people see you as being thoroughly prepared, they will be more likely to pass your name on to other qualified prospects. People like to help one another after a level of trust is earned.

It is not only important to prepare thoroughly before your sales meetings, but it is also very important to prepare as early as possible. One rule of thumb is that (if possible) you should try to prep for all meetings at least one week in advance. This way you will have a whole week to think about your presentation without being stressed out. This allows your subconscious mind to work on how to make the presentation the best it can be and also how you can add creativity into your meeting. You should then use the day before your meeting to do your final prepping and for getting in the right frame of mind.

> It is not only important to prepare thoroughly before your sales meetings, but it is also very important to prepare as early as possible.

Prepping early is critical for many reasons:

* *Early preparation gives you perspective and time to reflect.* When you prepare a week in advance, it gives your mind time to reflect on the subtle details of the upcoming presentation. You can spend the week before the meeting allowing new thoughts and ideas to come into your head, and you will have adequate time to act on them and customize your materials and sales plan. Each time you prepare and finish a task in preparation for your meeting, it frees up your mind to think of new thoughts about the sales process. If you only prepare the day before, your mind will not have time to think about the finer points of the game. Personally, I often think of three to four new things I can add to my presentation during the week leading up to

my pitches. They are frequently easy things to incorporate, but I know that I would not have thought of them if I were stressed out and trying to get the main parts of my presentation together the day before. It is the little things that impress a prospect and show that you care and were thinking about the prospect's individual situation. When you prepare and customize your presentation, it forces you to get inside the prospect's mind and think about ways in which he will use your products and services. This kind of preparation also makes prospects feel important. If you don't allow your mind the time to relax and get creative about your sales presentation, you won't come up with the kind of ideas that will win you business.

* ***Early preparation allows you to better customize your pitch.*** Preparing early also allows you to make multiple drafts of your sales presentation. Just like a writer who edits her work to craft her story over time, you must do the same. By being able to revisit your presentation over time, you will find you are able to see things more clearly with each new draft. Many times, something you thought would work quite well initially turns out not to work as well when you come back to it. Multiple iterations are critical for the flow of your presentation. Flow is the organization of topics you will be covering and is critical in making a winning presentation.

* ***Preparing early gives you more time to anticipate the prospect's needs.*** Preparing early also gives you more time to truly think about the prospect's needs. When you are preparing for a meeting, you will spend a lot of time just getting the basics of your pitch down. You need to set up your company overview, your presentation, your travel, coordination of other people, printing, etc. That's a lot of moving parts to worry about, and all of them need to get taken care of. The time allotted for anticipating prospect needs often comes last in the chain of preparation. By starting early, you will ensure that you have adequate time to think about the prospect's needs and identify the finer points that will wow him during the presentation.

* ***Preparing early is less stressful.*** It is less stressful when you prepare in advance. For most of us, making a sales presentation

is a rather anxious process. This is because selling combines three very stressful activities for most people: (1) public speaking, (2) salesmanship and, very often, (3) travel. When you are fully prepped in advance, it allows you to be more relaxed both the day before the meeting and the day of. Preparing early leaves you plenty of time to address any last-minute issues that come up (such as travel considerations, printing problems, and so on).

The competition in many sales situations is tough. Most prospects choose one firm over another due to only two or three reasons, and it can be even fewer for industries in which the product or service is more of a commodity. In these situations, it is really the finer points of the game that win you the business. If you think you are at your best under pressure, think again; you simply are not. It is always better to plan everything well in advance.

You should strive to be done preparing before lunchtime on the day before your presentation. View the preparation process as if you were striving to create a masterpiece. You will actually spend less time when you prepare in advance, so you might as well shift your schedule back a week and feel better and more relaxed.

Also, make sure you know as much about your prospect as possible. Perform a Google search on the company, and review any trade magazine articles. Visit their Web site. Use Google or LinkedIn to look up the people you will be seeing, and try to get to know something about them before you walk in the door. If you know someone at the target company, call him for information and get the lay of the land. Whatever it takes to be prepared, do it. It will pay off because prospects can tell when you've done your research, and it will differentiate you from the competition.

You will be able to tell when you have done a good job of preparing because prospects will tell you, either directly through words or through their body language. It is a great feeling when prospects give you a look of surprise at how prepared you are. Get to know this look and crave it in each presentation.

Being fully prepared early for each sales call will naturally help you overcome all of the common sales presentation issues we explored in

Chapter 7. Preparation also helps to endear each prospect to you, thereby improving your chances of obtaining more candid feedback about your sales process.

If you are staying up late the night before the meeting to get everything ready, you will often lose to another sales rep who is getting a good night's sleep.

PLAN TO BUILD RAPPORT

Once you are inside a prospect's office, the first thing you must do is build up some type of rapport. Many salespeople believe this to be a "luck of the draw" type of situation in which you will "click" with some people and not with others. We all know some salespeople who have a knack for getting along well with lots of different people. In fact, salespeople tend to be some of the most gregarious businesspeople, because they have to interact with many different types of people all the time. Salespeople tend to have a high emotional intelligence.

You have two options with respect to building rapport. The first option is to leave it to chance and hope each time that you can naturally build rapport with a prospect. This can work, and you will probably find that about 25 percent of the time you will hit it off with a prospect—you will like them and they will like you. Even a salesperson who is not highly skilled can win the business 25 percent of the time, perhaps because he is in the right place at the right time, the prospect needs what he is selling, or he has a good rapport with the prospect. This process occurs every day, and many salespeople play their careers like a numbers game. Now, some salespeople are able to get along with more than 25 percent of prospects and some less, but, over time, the only way to win more business is to see more people.

The second option takes this process to another level and attempts to control your rapport-building capabilities. Here are a few ways to improve rapport building with prospects:

* *Always have a plan B.* What I mean by this is that most salespeople just "wing it" with respect to building rapport. They

go in cold and attempt to make small talk with the prospect. This is their plan *A*. They don't plan anything and hope for the best. This gets even more complicated during team selling situations. Plan *A* is fine, but you must have a plan *B* ready in case you meet a prospect who is not interested in building rapport with you. We've all met prospects who make everything seem effortless, but we've also had prospects where everything feels stiff and with whom we lacked chemistry. The best way to get around this it to plan exactly what you are going to do if this situation occurs. You must have a plan *B* that you can go to right away so that you do not get flustered. Make sure you know what you'll say and where you'll go if you can't initially build rapport.

- *If you are selling to a group, plan your rapport building depending on different variations of who shows up first to the meeting.* This is an often overlooked problem that can occur at the beginning of a sales meeting. For instance, when you are selling to a group, the top decision maker will oftentimes arrive late to the meeting. I have found that the decision maker can sometimes arrive up to 10 minutes late to a meeting. Many times I am forced to make small talk with the others in the room before the meeting can get started. I'm sure many of you have had this happen. You must learn to turn this around and make it a positive. The way you do this is to plan your rapport-building questions for both situations (both when everyone shows up all at once as well as when the decision maker arrives late). Use this time to connect with committee members. Rapport can be built and much can be learned from prospects in the time it takes to set up your presentation.

- *When presenting to a group, find the committee member with whom you have the best connection (even if he is not the top decision maker). At the beginning of the presentation, focus on that person, smile, and make as much eye contact as possible.* This will help you warm up. When you build one solid connection, you will find other committee members picking up on it, and this will help you to develop a quicker rapport with the group as a whole. Once you've established one connection, move on to other audience members.

- *When in doubt, de-sell.* One other way to develop a stronger personal bond during the sales process is to actually pull back a little from the prospect and de-sell. As you saw in Chapter 7, prospects sometimes feel that salespeople are too aggressive and pushy, and they find that to be a turnoff. One way to get around this personal chemistry situation is to de-sell. What I mean by de-selling is that at some point during the sales process, you might try to backpedal a bit and test your prospect to see if he is truly interested in continuing the discussion. For example, you could say something like, "Mr. Prospect, I'm just wondering if our product is really a good fit for you. If it's not, that's OK too. We don't need to keep the dialogue going if it's not right for you." Then sit back and assess the prospect's reaction. If he takes the bait and wants to get out of the discussion, you should move on and close the sales process, because you don't have a serious prospect. However, if he reassures you that he is interested, he will try to make you feel better and often will reveal a piece of information that is holding him back from buying. Either way, this information will be valuable to you as a salesperson. When you give the prospect a chance to breathe, he will often realize how much he wants to buy and will chase you a little bit. This will help to strengthen your personal chemistry and rapport with each prospect.

As with any other skill in business, you can learn to get better at building rapport and developing chemistry with prospects. The key point is to find common ground, and the way you do that is by controlling the questions. The way to control the questions is to have them ready to use and be comfortable with having a backup strategy in case things don't seem natural. Don't just plan your sales presentation; plan your initial interaction with each prospect and rapport building. Lastly, if

> As with any other skill in business, you can learn to get better at building rapport and developing chemistry with prospects.

you get better at building rapport with each prospect, they will be more likely to be honest and candid with you not only throughout the sales process but also during your debrief.

UNDERSTAND YOUR PROSPECT'S UNIQUE NEEDS AND CUSTOMIZE YOUR PRESENTATION

> Your chances of success increase dramatically when you get a full understanding of what each prospect is looking for, because you will naturally be able to customize your sales process and presentation to each prospect's needs.

One of the best ways to improve your close rate is to work harder at making sure you fully understand each prospect's unique needs. Your chances of success increase dramatically when you get a full understanding of what each prospect is looking for, because you will naturally be able to customize your sales process and presentation to each prospect's needs.

Here are a few things you can do to learn each prospect's unique needs and better customize your presentations:

* *Develop a list of great open-ended sales questions to ask each prospect.* Every salesperson should have her own list of sales questions that focus on the prospect, the prospect's organization, and the prospect's business needs. For example, one great personal question to ask a prospect is, "How did you get into the business?" This question gets the prospect talking and allows you to learn about him as an individual and also see if you have any areas in common to build rapport. "How's business?" is a great organizational question that will allow you to get a reading on what the prospect's company is going through. Lastly, if you want to get more detail about a specific product or service need, you could ask, "What kinds of concerns do you have about product X/service Y/vendor Z? What is working? What is not working?" These questions are designed to get the prospect talking about the kinds of issues you need to be aware of as you try to sell him on a new solution. Asking questions is the only way to fully understand each prospect's needs and

customize your presentation, so always be prepared with a list of great sales questions.

- *Get each prospect talking.* Use questions to get prospects talking at the beginning of each sales process. It is absolutely critical to get them talking so you can learn what you need to know in order to provide them with solutions to their problems. One opening option is to start by saying, "Ms. Prospect, we have put together an agenda of what we would like to cover in today's meeting. However, before I start, can you take a few minutes to fill me in on what's important to you and what's going on with your current provider/product/service? This will help me clarify and better tailor my remarks as we go through the meeting." These efforts will help you better understand each prospect's unique needs and customize your presentation accordingly.

- *Always restate or paraphrase each prospect's unique needs before you present your solution.* This will not only show the prospect that you listened but will also allow him to correct you if you are off in any areas.

- *Take notes.* As we reviewed earlier, when you take notes, it makes the prospect feel important and serves to keep him talking. It will also help you to organize your thinking and make sure you don't forget anything throughout your sales process.

- *Customize your pitch.* Once you have correctly and thoroughly assessed your prospect's key decision-making criteria, you must apply this knowledge to your presentation. Make sure your presentation covers each of the hot button issues that the prospect revealed to you during the early identifying needs portion of your sales meeting. Do not worry if your sales materials do not reflect this customization; just try to show the prospect that you understand what she is looking for and address each of her areas of interest.

- *Be consultative.* Once the prospect has opened up about his true needs, you should then be consultative in your sales approach. This is where being a product expert comes into play. When you position yourself as a consultant or expert (and not just as a salesperson), you will get much further with prospects, but you have to know what they are looking for before you can do this, and you have to be an expert in your product, service, and industry. All you need to do is consult with them on what the best solution is to their problem. Here's an important point: If your product or service is not what they are looking for, point them in the right direction for their needs. Don't try to force your company on them. You will find that this simple act will actually make your prospect more likely to accept what you have to offer. Prospects are always thankful for a salesperson who is trying to do right by them as opposed to someone who is just in it for a quick sale. Be consultative. Pretend that each prospect is a family member you are advising.

- *Even if you have a good idea of the prospect's key decision-making criteria before going into the presentation, these criteria may have changed as other providers presented their solutions before you.* Therefore, it is important to get the prospect talking early and to remain flexible throughout the presentation.

Just as a salesperson should never try to close a sale before presenting a solution, a sales rep should be careful when trying to make a presentation before fully establishing rapport or understanding the prospect's needs. Remember, when the flow of the sales process is broken, it can diminish your chances of winning the business.

Obviously when you work hard at understanding what each prospect is looking for, you will be in a much better position to make the sale, but you will also be better off when you debrief with prospects at the end of the sales process. You will have a much better understanding of all the key decision-making criteria, which will allow you to more skillfully debrief with each prospect regarding each salient issue.

MAKE EACH PROSPECT FEEL IMPORTANT

As we explored in Chapter 7, making prospects feel important is an often overlooked aspect of the sales process. In fact, most sales training and sales books overlook this as a critical reason that salespeople lose business.

Here are a few ways you can make prospects feel important:

- *Return prospect phone calls within 24 hours or, better yet, within 2 hours.* Responsiveness is absolutely critical during the sales process, and it goes a long way toward showing prospects how much you care about them and their business. No prospect has ever said, "That salesperson got back to me too quickly, so I did not give her the business." The quicker you call prospects back to answer questions, the more they will take notice, leaving a positive impression. Remember, if you take a long time to call prospects back, they will go with other salespeople who are more responsive. Another reason responsiveness is so important in making a prospect feel valued is that prospects infer from the salesperson's performance the type of customer service they will receive from an organization. Think about it: before a prospect becomes a customer, his main way of assessing how he'll be treated as a customer is by how the salesperson interacts with him and how quickly he is called back. If the prospect does not feel important during the sales process, he typically believes he will not be valued as a customer.

- *If a prospect leaves you a message and asks a question you do not know the answer to, do not wait a long time to call her back to get her the answer.* Instead, call the prospect back to let her know that you are working on it and that you will get back to her as soon as you have an answer. Prospects respect this method because most of the time, they just want to know you are working on the situation.

- *When you are out of the office, forward calls to your cell phone.* Very few salespeople do this. Think about the positive message it sends to the prospect that you are willing to take calls when you are on the road. Prospects want to give the business to whomever they see working the hardest, and when you forward your calls, you will be more accessible to your prospects. Additionally, you will not need to play phone tag, which saves you and the prospect a lot of time and frustration. Call your phone company and set up this functionality today.

- *Make sure you are 100 percent enthusiastic about the product or service you are selling.* If you are not excited about what you are doing, move into a new field or change jobs and go to work for a firm that you are more excited about. A large part of making a prospect feel important is transferred through your own ability to show enthusiasm for what you are doing. If you are not excited about your company and about what it can do for the prospect, many times the prospect will take this as a sign that you do not care about them.

- *Never tell a prospect you are on vacation, at lunch, or busy with a colleague (even if you are).* The only reason you should ever be unavailable to a prospect is because you are with another customer. Tell all of your support people that if a prospect cannot get in touch with you, they should tell the prospect you are with another customer. Not a prospect, a customer.

If you apply these types of responsiveness tactics in your daily interactions with prospects, you will ameliorate many of the common sales issues related to making prospects feel important (discussed in Chapter 7). When prospects see you as responsive, they will never perceive that you are arrogant or that you are just in it for the commission check. Even if your company is large, it will make them feel valued by you and ultimately by your company.

Additionally, if you make all of your prospects feel important, whether you win or lose, they will be more likely to give you more candid and accurate feedback during your postdecision debriefs.

COMMIT TO BECOMING AN EXPERT IN YOUR FIELD

Another critical step toward improving your new business win rate (and your ability to understand why you win and lose) is to increase your knowledge. You must become focused on learning everything you can about your product or service, as well as everything about your competition and the industry you are in. If you are not 100 percent interested

> If you are not 100 percent interested in what you are selling, it will come through in your relations with prospects.

in what you are selling, it will come through in your relations with prospects. Make sure you are passionate about what you are doing; otherwise, it is difficult for prospects to become interested in your product, company, or industry.

There are four keys areas in which salespeople must continually improve their knowledge:

- *Product/service knowledge.* You must learn everything you can about the product or service you are selling. You should strive to make yourself an expert in your field. People want to buy from experts, not salespeople. You should seek to establish yourself as a consultant, not just a salesperson. High levels of product and service knowledge allow you to feel more confident

  > **People want to buy from experts, not salespeople.**

  in front of prospects, which will help you in all areas of the sales process. Additionally, when you know a lot about what you are selling, you will inherently become more enthusiastic, which will help you significantly when in front of customers. Product knowledge will also help you with objection handling. Always be up to speed on new features that your products or services provide. Attend as much product training as possible.
- *Industry knowledge.* You also must become an expert in your industry. Read all of the trade magazines on a consistent basis so you fully understand everything that is going on in your field. This will make you come across as more worldly in your interactions with prospects, and it will allow you to have more detailed discussions with them during the sales process. This will help you to build rapport with prospects.
- *Competitive knowledge.* You should also understand your competition thoroughly. You must know where they are strong and weak so you can best compete against them. Study your competition. Your win/loss interviews will help you significantly, but don't stop there. Any competitive information you can gather must be used to help you learn how to differentiate yourself and your company from the competition. The only way you can differentiate your company from competitors is if you know a

lot about the companies you are selling against. Differentiating yourself during the sales process is one of the finer points of salesmanship. This skill set comes with experience and maturity, because it is difficult to talk knowledgeably about how you are different from the competition if you are not an expert on the competitive landscape. It should be stressed, however, that you should never disparage the competition when you are in the process of discussing how you are different. This is a big mistake and a real turnoff for prospects. When I see a salesperson disparage his competition, it is often a sign of inexperience. If you are a highly skilled professional, you should be able to convey how you are different from your competition without being negative. In fact, you should welcome when prospects ask you how you are different, because it gives you the chance to clearly articulate your value proposition, and most prospects will believe what you say.

> The only way you can differentiate your company from competitors is if you know a lot about the companies you are selling against.

- **Sales process knowledge.** Lastly, you must keep learning about selling and the sales process itself. Sales is a lifelong career, and there is as much to learn as there is in any other career. You can always develop yourself and get better at your profession. Read more sales books, listen to audio programs, or attend sales training and seminars. These educational outlets will also be much more effective once you implement the win/loss program in this book because you will be much more informed of the critical areas you personally need to work on.

It was Albert Einstein who once said, "Insanity is doing the same thing over and over again and expecting different results." So ask yourself, are you performing the same sales process over and over again, year after year, and expecting a different result? If you answer yes to this question, then it's time to do some more learning in your field in order to gain fresh insights into your marketplace, products, services, and sales process.

If you become an expert in your field, you will never starve. Very few business people become experts at anything because most people haven't sought out or found their true callings in their work. Make sure you are building your foundation in the right career path and industry; it will make your efforts at becoming an expert much easier and more fruitful.

OBTAIN CUSTOMER TESTIMONIALS

One valuable by-product of debriefing with and learning from bids won customers is that you will be in a much better position to talk about these positive situations during subsequent sales calls. It is always valuable to be able to talk to prospects about happy customers, and the more you understand why people chose you and your firm, the better you will be at articulating it in future sales situations.

Use these discussions to gather client testimonials for use in future sales situations. Written client testimonials can be a valuable tool in your sales process arsenal, and you should gather these from new and existing clients. Ask your new clients to write two to three sentences on why they chose you and your firm's products and services.

Obtaining client testimonials from customers that you have sold will give you fresh insights into why prospects buy from you, what they like about you as a salesperson, and why they chose your company's products and services. This will allow you to enhance your strengths during future sales situations. It will also allow you to understand how you were able to successfully overcome any obstacles that might have stood in your way.

One complaint I have heard in many sales organizations is that salespeople have a difficult time obtaining references from the client service side. My response has always been that if this is the case, you should take control of the situation and create your own references (if your company will allow it). There is nothing wrong with using your own bids won prospects as personal references, and written client testimonials are a great starting point for developing an ongoing relationship for a business reference.

Lastly, as you know, sales can be a discouraging business. You face a lot of rejection on a daily basis, so it is important to take the time to speak with current customers you have sold so you can gain motivation and encouragement from these situations. It is a great way to connect and keep your relationship going with customers, so don't be afraid to ask for client testimonials and use them during your sales process.

CHAPTER WRAP-UP

All of the techniques in this chapter are designed to help you refine your sales skills and to help you improve your sales effectiveness. These ideas are also designed to help you get more candid information from prospects when you debrief with them postdecision, because one of the best ways to get the most candid information is to be the best salesperson you can be. Once you become a consummate professional, your prospects will treat you with more respect at all times.

By implementing the tactics in this chapter, you will eliminate many of the common sales deficiencies cited by prospects, and you will essentially remove them as reservations during the sales process. Therefore, as you diminish the amount of "sales defects" within each sales process, prospects in general will be more open with you both during and at the end of your sales cycle. The best way to get candid feedback is to be the best at what you do. Prospects can sense when something is well done. For example, people can tell when you are prepared and when you are not, and they can pick up on when you feel they are important or not.

> When you commit to total quality in all of your interactions with prospects, they in turn will be more likely to want to help you succeed.

When you commit to total quality in all of your interactions with prospects, they in turn will be more likely to want to help you succeed. They will also be more willing to take a chance on your product or service because they will believe in you and your enthusiasm. When you commit to becoming an expert in your field, prospects will be drawn to you, and you will be better able to discern what you need to do to succeed in each new business situation.

Lastly, when you focus on getting to and selling to the actual decision maker, your sales effectiveness will rise because you will be selling to the right person. This will speed up your sales process, and you will also receive more candid and accurate feedback about how your products and services are truly being used. You will also generally get more candid feedback because the people who make it into decision-making roles are generally some of the best communicators within a company and are the most skilled at making decisions.

Sales is the top profession in business because generating revenue and getting customers will always be the most important part of any business. Businesses cease to exist unless they have customers, and customers come from salespeople. This is why it is so important for you as a salesperson to continually work on your craft and become the best salesperson you can be.

CHAPTER SUMMARY

The following sales techniques will help you better understand why you win and lose and will help you win more business:

* Track your close rate.
* Always sell to the decision maker; start at the top.
* Prepare, prepare, prepare (and prepare early, not the day before).
* Plan to build rapport.
* Understand your prospect's unique needs, and customize your presentation.
* Make prospects feel important by showing them that you want their business.
* Increase your sales, product, service, and industry knowledge by committing to becoming an expert in your field.
* Obtain client testimonials.

Conclusion

As my father once told me, "If you can sell and become a rainmaker, everyone will leave you alone. If you can close business, no one will care what school you went to, what time you get to work, how you dress, or how you act." This is why sales is the great equalizer in business. Top salespeople come from all walks of life, and it does not matter whether you have an "academic pedigree" or not. In sales, there is nothing holding you back from achieving except yourself, but you do have to work on your craft in order to earn the moniker of "rainmaker."

If you implement the techniques in this book, you will improve your sales performance, but the improvements will come with time—nothing happens overnight in life or in business. Real change comes the old fashioned way, bit by bit, day by day, and year by year. I hope this program showed you how to develop a system that will allow you to make incremental changes along the way so you can work on constantly improving your skills as a sales professional.

The very best salespeople focus on refining their sales process every day, but as you continue to focus on winning, make sure you also celebrate your improvements along the way. The journey is just as important as the end result.

Thank you for reading this book. I hope this program helps you become more successful in the future.

All the best.

Why You Should Implement a Win/Loss Program for Your Sales Team

In Appendixes A and B, we will review one final approach that can help sales teams overcome all the obstacles addressed in this book, as well as many additional organizational challenges that often stem from collecting win/loss feedback through individual salespeople. Although the focus of this book is on helping any salesperson improve how he individually debriefs with prospects postdecision, there are also benefits and synergies to implementing a formal win/loss program across an entire sales team.

The purpose of a more formal win/loss analysis program is to gather competitive intelligence and aggregated feedback on your company's products/services and sales process, which you can use to improve your sales team's performance in the future. This type of program focuses on all the members of your sales team, not just on one individual salesperson. Therefore, these appendixes are intended for anyone who is involved in managing a sales team, who is responsible for running a business that oversees a sales force, or who is part of a senior management team that is involved with and impacted by a sales organization. Product, marketing, and research managers will also find these appendixes to be of value.

Over the last 15 years, a growing number of companies have been implementing formal win/loss analysis programs, often hiring independent, outside parties to conduct the interviews on behalf of

Over the last 15 years, a growing number of companies have been implementing formal win/loss analysis programs, often hiring independent, outside parties to conduct the interviews on behalf of all members of their sales teams.

all members of their sales teams. By using an independent third party to conduct the debriefs, sales teams and companies can learn the true, candid reasons they win and lose and circumvent the interpersonal relationship issues we explored in Chapters 2 and 3. Unfortunately, at present, less than 18 percent of companies have implemented a formal program, which means that a large number of companies are missing out on the immense benefits of this unique management tool.

Before you decide to implement a win/loss analysis program for your company, you should first understand all of the benefits. In Appendix A, I will show you why a formal win/loss analysis program can be a critical tool in helping your sales team increase its new business win rate and improve the strategic functioning of your organization. This chapter will also show why it is critical for all companies to gather and disseminate this type of feedback throughout the organization in order to help enhance their products, services, sales process, pricing, marketing, technology, and positioning strategy.

Appendix A has four sections. First, we will explore the inherent challenges that typical companies face as sales teams turn inward to share their marketplace knowledge and win/loss prospect feedback. Second, we will explore the organizational challenges that arise as faulty prospect feedback circulates throughout a company, with each area putting its own unique spin on key issues and problems. Third, we will explore how this common organizational behavior often leads to strategic misalignment. Lastly, we will review all the benefits of implementing a formal institutional win/loss program. By the time you finish reading this appendix, you will realize that for successful companies, a win/loss analysis program is not discretionary.

Let's begin by exploring a few inherent organizational challenges that stem from relying solely on salespeople to capture and disseminate win/loss feedback.

THE CHALLENGES OF GATHERING PROSPECT FEEDBACK WITHOUT A FORMAL MECHANISM

As we explored in Chapters 2 and 3, salespeople are not in the most objective position to gather feedback, and prospects are typically not candid. This is the first set of challenges that many organizations face when assessing their competitive positioning. However, all of these issues are exacerbated when fragmented and often faulty prospect feedback is sporadically spread throughout a larger organization.

Before we explore all the organizational challenges that stem from these issues, let's review the reasons prospects are typically not forthcoming and ways in which salespeople inhibit the feedback process:

Reasons for Prospects Not Being Forthcoming and Candid

* Prospects often feel uncomfortable giving feedback and criticism directly to salespeople because they do not want to hurt their feelings.
* Prospects often fear confrontation or criticism from sales reps who can become defensive while receiving feedback.
* Prospects don't spend a lot of time with salespeople to give them bad news.
* Prospects often have issues with the sales rep or sales process that can impact their candor.
* The real reasons for loss may make the prospect look bad.
* Prospects may feel reluctant to provide too much information on their chosen vendors.

Ways in Which Salespeople Inhibit the Feedback Process

* Salespeople are not in an objective position to obtain feedback.
* Salespeople may be caught off guard by a bad news call and therefore are often unprepared for conducting a debrief.
* Salespeople usually do not know the right questions to ask (and how to ask them) because most sales professionals have historically overlooked and poorly utilized prospect debriefs.

- Salespeople typically do not debrief with bids won prospects to better understand why they won (and what they can do better).
- It can be very difficult to ascertain the true reasons for loss if you are not selling directly to the decision maker.
- When salespeople sell through intermediaries, channels, or partners, it can often be difficult to have direct contact with the end prospect and gather any meaningful postdecision feedback.

There are many challenges salespeople need to overcome in order to gather more candid feedback from prospects postdecision. Many of these obstacles can be overcome by implementing the techniques in this book; however, the truth of the matter is that most salespeople will not learn how to obtain honest and accurate feedback from prospects. Even if a few salespeople on your sales team learn these techniques, the rest will remain uneducated about this critical final element of the sales process. Therefore, there will always be inconsistency with respect to how each sales team member approaches debriefing with prospects.

This situation is challenging for anyone who is leading a sales team or running a company. Not only do sales teams and sales managers face all the individual challenges outlined above (and in Chapters 2 and 3), but they also need to deal with all the inconsistency inherent in letting each sales team member debrief in his or her own unique way. Just as some salespeople have a higher close rate than others, some salespeople will be better at debriefing with prospects than others. This consistency issue causes problems when a sales team and company try to assess their aggregate strengths and weaknesses.

> There will always be inconsistency with respect to how each sales team member approaches debriefing with prospects.

Additionally, because sales teams typically do not have a full, unbiased understanding of why they win and lose, they often unknowingly disseminate incomplete or inaccurate information within their organizations. Since 60 percent of the time salespeople do not get an accurate depiction of why they lose, it would stand to reason that prospect information being circulated around most companies is inexact the majority of the time. This often misleads other departments and can compromise decision making.

Compounding this problem is the fact that salespeople are typically less likely to pass on critical feedback regarding their own performance during the sales process. How often do you hear a salesperson say, "The reason we lost is because I could have done a better job at selling"? Salespeople will not typically blame themselves for lost deals. As we explored, most prospects will not criticize the salesperson directly; therefore, salespeople understate their own deficiencies because they are often unaware of them. Feedback can easily become more focused on other areas of the company (such as pricing, product features, branding, and so on) and may not reflect an accurate proportioning of the true issues.

Salespeople are out with customers and prospects all the time; they do tend to develop a keen sense of what is going on in the marketplace, and they are often the first to hear about new enhancements being made by the competition. Depending on a company's organizational structure, it may be the sales team's job to educate the rest of the company on what is going on in the marketplace, because sales is often in the best position to identify new trends. However, in many companies, this information is primarily stored inside the salesperson's head. Salespeople possess a wealth of information, but companies don't often take the steps necessary to exploit the full extent of their knowledge (and salespeople don't always provide all of the details because their job is to keep selling).

Additionally, depending on the average tenure of each salesperson on a sales team, each individual salesperson may have varying degrees of knowledge about a wide range of industry and product subjects. The challenge becomes how to funnel this information to other areas of the company that need direct access to it. Factoring in that salespeople get paid to sell, not to educate the rest of the company on what is going on in the marketplace, it is easy to see how barriers get created. Also, many salespeople get desensitized to the fact that they may know a lot more than the rest of the company and assume that everyone knows what they know.

Another strategic challenge of relying on individual salespeople for competitive intelligence is that there may be broader trends that a salesperson cannot discern individually. Take for example a large organization that competes with a leading competitor many times throughout the year. If this competitor has recently instituted a more competitive pricing model, it could be assumed that the salespeople would pick up on it. The problem is that if you have many salespeople and each has witnessed the new pricing only once, they might have thought the pricing was an anomaly. However, this information in aggregate would clearly outline a trend and enable the company to better position itself against this competitor.

> Another strategic challenge of relying on individual salespeople for competitive intelligence is that there may be broader trends that a salesperson cannot discern individually.

The most efficient and effective way to ensure that deficiencies exposed in the field are shared throughout the organization is through independent and comprehensive verification. In effect, a thorough win/loss analysis program managed by an outside third party provides a means for getting prospect information out of salespeople's heads and to the rest of the organization. (It also allows salespeople to do what they do best: generate sales.)

Now that we have explored the organizational challenges of using salespeople as a starting point for information gathering, let's address how this process often sets off a chain reaction that limits information sharing and hinders learning and sound decision making across different areas of a company.

THE ORGANIZATIONAL CHALLENGES OF PROSPECT FEEDBACK INFORMATION SHARING

As faulty prospect feedback and information spread throughout companies, it ultimately corrupts decision making. Over time, senior managers start making decisions based on inaccurate information derived from prospects who were not fully candid and salespeople who are not in a truly objective position to share unbiased information.

> As faulty prospect feedback and information spread throughout companies, it ultimately corrupts decision making.

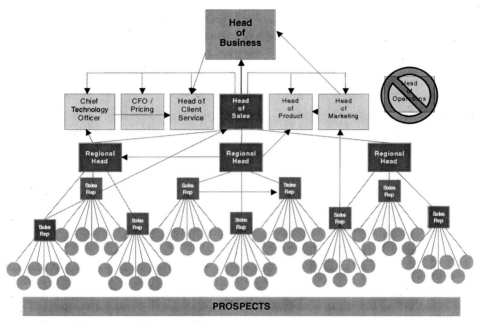

Figure A.1   Internal Information Paths

To start, let's explore how prospect and sales information typically gets passed up the chain of command in most organizations. First, the prospect tells the salesperson why the deal was won or lost. The salesperson then tells her regional sales manager. The sales manager then tells the head of sales, and the head of sales might aggregate this information and relay it to the executive management team. Although information sharing is not this rigid in all companies, there is generally a hierarchy through which information travels.

As you can see from Figure A.1, information typically spreads in sporadic ways. A salesperson may relay information to her regional sales head, or she may bump into the head of marketing in the hallway and discuss some information. There is usually no clear process for capturing and relaying this information company-wide. Additionally, as new people hear and digest the information, they inadvertently incorporate their own biases and experience levels into the feedback, thereby putting their own unique spins on the message, and so with each new person, the story changes. Additionally, some areas of the company may not receive any feedback (in Figure A.1, for example, that area would be operations).

As reviewed in Chapter 3, this type of communication pattern is analogous to the telephone whisper game often played by children. By the time any prospect feedback makes its way around a company, the message is watered down and most likely quite different from what the prospect originally said. The inefficiency of this model is especially pronounced in companies with larger sales teams where information paths inevitably get longer and harder to maintain. Since information is power, corporate politics and bureaucracy can also play a role in hindering the flow of information through a company.

> By the time any prospect feedback makes its way around a company, the message is watered down and most likely quite different from what the prospect originally said.

Given that companies are already starting at a disadvantage because prospects tell salespeople the full and candid truth only 40 percent of the time, and adding in the further complexity that information is being gathered and shared by numerous salespeople, each with his or her own individual biases (and experience levels with respect to debriefing with prospects), it is easy to see how organizations often make decisions on much more limited information than they'd like to admit.

Hierarchical factors can also inhibit the flow of information (especially up to a company's senior management team), as not all employees feel comfortable discussing and debating problems with senior management. Therefore, information (especially negative and problem information) does not always get shared with company leaders. Many employees are more worried about the leader's opinion and may be selective in their information sharing and feedback about what needs to be done at the company. Some employees concern themselves only with making sure they are pleasing the leader as opposed to developing and voicing their own opinions.

This issue compounds when companies have a leader who is not accepting of others' opinions. Some companies have self-absorbed or tyrannical leaders, and in these cases, it may be hard for employees to voice their own opinions. If intimidation is used by a leader, it can limit information sharing and the critical debate and dialogue about what needs to be done to keep pace in the marketplace. Employees may be too fearful about what the leader will think and may choose not to bring information forward.

Figure A.2 depicts the same situation for a company that conducts win/loss analysis in a more formal manner with an outside third party. While maintaining direct lines of communication with the salesperson remains an important part of the process, a better way to gather information from the front lines is to have someone who is uninvolved in the sales process speak directly to prospects. When win/loss information is captured by an independent third party, the chain of command stays intact, but information sharing is more widely distributed and, most important, the information is consistent at every level. The information does not change as it moves around the organization. The feedback stays true and does not become affected by the various spins and biases within the organization.

In one sense, win/loss analysis allows the head of sales and the senior management team of a company to effectively be "out in the field"

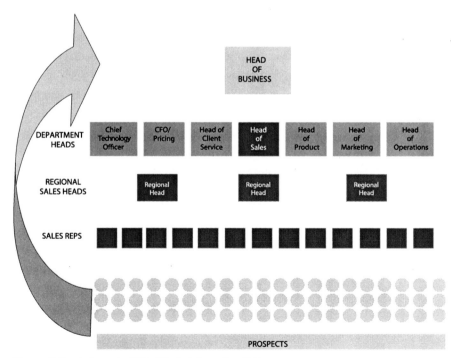

Figure A.2   Independent Third-Party Information Path

on each deal. By getting a complete independent transcript of each deal situation, senior managers can feel as though they have a pulse on their sales teams' efforts and on the marketplace.

Although it is true that each person within the organization will tend to put his own spin on the independent data and some may attempt to control it, at least all employees will be working off the same accurate starting point. Additionally, in situations where an outside party gathers the data, it will be harder for internal biases and spins to corrupt the findings. This helps organizations better understand themselves and therefore make better ongoing strategic decisions.

In the next section, we will take this analysis one step further as we explore how this typical organizational process ultimately leads to strategic misalignment.

GARBAGE IN, GARBAGE OUT: WHY COMPANIES SUFFER FROM STRATEGIC MISALIGNMENT

Each of the organizational issues reviewed in this appendix are problems unto themselves, but collectively they lead to the last and perhaps most damaging situation for any company: strategic misalignment. The more a company becomes misaligned with its customers, prospects, and marketplace, the harder it can be to catch up to industry leaders.

Not understanding what prospects are looking for and not having this information readily available can create significant strategic misalignment in your company's products, services, pricing, sales process, marketing/branding, and strategy. Due to this common breakdown in properly gathering and understanding unbiased information from prospects, most companies suffer from some form of misalignment. When a company suffers from misalignment in many of these areas, it becomes difficult to implement a well-tailored growth strategy.

> Not understanding what prospects are looking for and not having this information readily available can create significant strategic misalignment.

Many companies focus too much energy internally and lose touch with

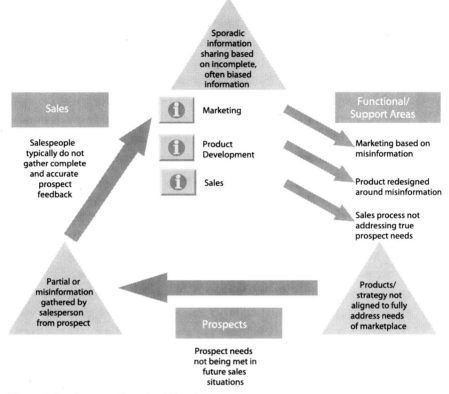

Figure A.3   Corporate Triangle of Misinformation

their marketplace. When a company is out of alignment with the marketplace, it will eventually fall prey to a competitor that is more in touch with what prospects and customers need and want. Companies that acquire this type of information in a systematic, consistent manner over time can develop a strategic advantage over weaker competitors.

Figure A.3 explores the typical corporate triangle of misinformation that leads to strategic misalignment in many companies. Salespeople rarely get complete and accurate information from prospects, which leads to a situation where inaccurate information gets shared sporadically and inefficiently throughout an organization. This can culminate in a misaligned strategy in many functional areas of a corporation.

In Figure A.3, salespeople feed incomplete prospect and market-place information to different areas of the company (i.e., marketing, product development, and sales). Each of these areas begins to make decisions and alter strategies based on incomplete or faulty information. Thus, the company's strategy becomes misaligned with the needs of the marketplace, which in turn impacts the sales team and prospects in future new business situations. As this scenario perpetuates, companies can move further and further down a spiral of misalignment that can lead to less than optimal performance. As the old computer programming saying goes, "Garbage in, garbage out."

A company's products and services are the most critical element that can be impacted by misalignment. The best way to learn how to enhance your company's product or service is to not only listen to your customers but also to your prospects. Prospects are an even better source of feedback than current customers. When you speak to a prospect after a recent buying decision has been made, you are talking directly to someone who has just evaluated not only your company's products and services but also those of your competitors. Additionally, if prospects are switching to a new product or service, they will also have the hindsight of working with another competitor. Therefore, they are an exceptional source of buyer behavior and knowledge about the marketplace and industry.

Since prospects are not yet clients, they primarily base their decisions on their perceptions of your company. Unlike current clients, who already have experience working with your company, prospects are able to provide perceptions of your products and services. Perceptions are important to understand because they provide a good gauge of how the marketplace thinks and feels about your company. It is important to identify marketplace perceptions so that your marketing and branding strategies can accentuate company strengths while counteracting any negative perceptions.

Similar to better understanding your company's products and services, feedback on your company's technological capabilities can also be a useful tool. Technology areas often get very specific feedback from current customers, but what about from prospects? Prospect feedback can be much more telling because it links into the market-place and the competition. Prospects are often in a great position to comment about a company's technology because they are coming from another vendor and can provide feedback with the benefit of prior experience. In today's ever-changing world, keeping pace with technology is not a luxury but rather a critical component of any company's success.

If companies don't listen to prospects and seek their feedback, they will eventually find themselves behind the marketplace with respect to the quality of their products and services. Thus, companies can find themselves misaligned with the marketplace.

In contrast to the typical flow of information explored in this chapter, when win/loss is conducted independently by an outside firm, each area of a company can have a say in the design of the debrief questionnaire and be on the distribution list of interviews. Additionally, each functional area of a company can analyze the aggregated analysis reporting of all the data. This means that these areas will be able to tap into the marketplace and better understand what prospects are saying about their products and services.

As this feedback loop perpetuates over time, sales, product, and service managers can begin to make more informed decisions. These decisions will now be influenced by true prospect feedback and will therefore be more strategically aligned to the needs of the marketplace. Once a successful win/loss program begins to facilitate information sharing company-wide, a virtuous cycle of continuous improvement can replace the negative spiral of misinformation described earlier.

Now that we have reviewed the organizational challenges present in companies lacking a formal win/loss analysis process, let's review the benefits that come from implementing a formal win/loss analysis program.

THE BENEFITS OF IMPLEMENTING A FORMAL WIN/LOSS ANALYSIS PROGRAM

The most important long-term goal and benefit of making a win/loss analysis program a part of your organization's process is to increase your company's new business win rate. This is achieved through an improved understanding of how your sales team and your company's products and services compare with the competition. Other benefits include:

- Understand the candid reasons prospects buy and don't buy from your company (across your entire sales team).
- Identify your company's strengths and weaknesses.
- Improve the effectiveness of your company's sales presentations and sales team.
- Develop an organic training program by allowing each salesperson to apply feedback to all areas of his or her sales process.
- Use prospect feedback as a training and performance evaluation tool for sales and other presentation team personnel.
- Implement tactics that are more effective and actionable than typical sales training.
- Uncover unmet prospect/customer needs.
- Identify prospect perceptions of the strengths and weaknesses of your products and services.
- Formally share prospect perceptions across all areas of your organization to enhance product and service development.
- Benchmark your company's performance against the competition.

By understanding exactly where your company stands in the eyes of prospects, your sales team will be in a better position to execute more successfully during the sales process. A formal win/loss analysis program will also help all of your salespeople calibrate their views of their own sales performance versus those of their prospects. As detailed in Chapter 2, the average salesperson believes his personal performance is to blame only 25 percent of the time when he loses a deal, and he believes he is a major reason a deal is won 75 percent of the time. By reading actual candid prospect feedback, salespeople can learn how prospects truly view their sales performance.

This form of calibration is really what win/loss is all about. One reason salespeople have misconceptions about their own abilities is that they are typically not overseen by managers on a day to day basis. When regional territories are a necessity, it means that salespeople often work out of their homes. They also sell mostly on their own, without much supervision (unless they are involved in more complex sales situations/team selling). Therefore, salespeople get less feedback on their performance compared to other corporate workers. Salespeople are generally managed with a "sink or swim" mentality, and this is one reason we often see that salespeople do not have a totally accurate perception of themselves. A win/loss program can serve as a valuable training and feedback tool that is missing from many sales teams.

It is only through healthy and constructive feedback that a sales manager can calibrate each sales team member's opinion of his sales performance with those of his prospects, but it requires a formal third-party mechanism to accomplish this. Implementing this kind of formal mechanism is what most sales teams never do, and they stagnate in their own limitations as a result.

A career in sales requires a commitment to self-improvement. Salespeople tend to be highly competitive and motivated. Not only are they more able than most to push themselves to perform better, but their peers are also pushing themselves every day as well. It requires constant effort just to keep pace with the competition. One of the best ways to institutionalize and harness this effort is by committing your sales team to an ongoing commitment to candid feedback on their sales performance.

Let's face it, on average, a salesperson or sales team will be lucky to have a close ratio of 40 percent. This means that even a successful salesperson or team will face rejection 60 percent of the time. However, even if your sales team's close rate is 40 percent, there is still a lot of opportunity to improve and gain market share. The truth of the matter is that you are already spending time and money on the other 60 percent of the situations you are involved in. Therefore, if you could just figure out how to get more wins out of that 60 percent, your company would be a whole lot better off. Many companies never invest in finding out the true reasons they are winning and losing and are never able to implement the right tactics to increase their new business win rate.

If you dig down even further, you will find that average close rates can be deceiving, because each salesperson has her own close rate. We all know that in each sales team, there are stars as well as average and below average salespeople. Stars may close 50 to 60 percent while the below average salesperson might close 20 percent. Win/loss reviews can formalize the process by which less experienced salespeople learn from more experienced ones.

It takes the same amount of time to be successful at selling as it does to fail at sales. All salespeople have the same number of hours each day to work, so at a certain point, differentiation comes from how salespeople allocate their time. The reason top performers are successful is that they continuously refine their salesmanship abilities and ultimately get more yield out of their time. Remember, someone who makes a million dollars a year has the exact same amount of time as someone who makes $50,000 a year. The way to make more money is to improve on what you do, and the quickest way to improve on what you do is to learn from prospects why you win and lose and then act on the feedback.

Win/loss analysis offers companies a significant accumulative advantage over the competition, the benefits of which can grow substantially over time. By committing to a continuous and unbiased prospect feedback loop that can be shared across all areas of an organization, companies can more accurately make enhancements at all levels. Over time, this management tool can allow a company to charge ahead of its competition by continually keeping a pulse on industry trends, the competition, and needed enhancements to the sales process, products, and services.

> Win/loss analysis offers companies a significant accumulative advantage over the competition, the benefits of which can grow substantially over time.

APPENDIX WRAP-UP

Growing a company requires working with prospects. All of the issues mentioned in Appendix A prevent companies from fully understanding their prospects, and this is a dangerous proposition since prospects represent where a company is going. The good news is that this situation can be rectified by incorporating a new and critical element into your team's sales process: a formal, independent win/loss analysis program.

An institutional win/loss analysis program serves as a solution to the organizational problems explored in this appendix (as well as the issues explored

> **Growing a company requires working with prospects.**

in Chapters 2 and 3). First, win/loss reviews allow each salesperson (and an entire sales team) to get a full and accurate debrief on each select sales situation. By collecting and aggregating this data, your entire sales team can fully understand why it wins and loses in new business situations and begin to make the necessary changes to its sales process to increase the company's new business win rate. This process stands in stark contrast to the typical way most companies try to get feedback from prospects, by relying on the sales team to gather this data.

Second, because there will be in-depth telephone conversations with each prospect and resulting interview transcripts, your company can use these transcripts to more accurately disseminate data throughout the organization. By using a clearly defined interview distribution system, different areas of your company can tap into the vast knowledge and "storage facility" of prospect feedback. Your sales team will no longer need to be solely responsible for supplying prospect and marketplace feedback, and the inherent conflict of interest will subside.

Additionally, quarterly or annual reporting of win/loss results can be used to aggregate real time data and present the findings to all areas of the company in a clear and concise way. By committing to the process of sharing unbiased, candid prospect feedback with many areas of your company, your employees will no longer need to play "the telephone whisper game." This will mean that now everyone in your company is getting the same straight feedback and information in a consistent way, all at the same time.

Last, each employee in each area of your company can begin to make better and more informed decisions on a daily basis. This will help to enhance your company's products and/or services, pricing, marketing, technology, customer service, and strategy. This will serve to better align each of these key areas with the needs of the marketplace and will help your company better compete.

Now that we have explored the organizational challenges companies can face when they do not have a strong system for gathering and aggregating prospect feedback, we will move to Appendix B and show you how to implement a formal, institutional win/loss analysis program. By learning how to build a successful program, your company will develop a strategic advantage in the marketplace because your strategy will become much more aligned with what prospects are looking for.

APPENDIX SUMMARY

The Challenges of Gathering Prospect Feedback without a Formal Mechanism

Five challenges exist when salespeople gather and share marketplace information throughout their organization:

- There will always be inconsistency with respect to how each sales team member approaches debriefing with prospects.
- Incomplete and/or inaccurate information is disseminated throughout the organization because salespeople often do not have an accurate sense of why they win and lose.
- Critical information regarding the sales team's performance is rarely shared, creating disproportionate and faulty feedback loops.
- Competitive intelligence gained in the field is often stored inside the salesperson's head. (Salespeople get paid to sell, not to educate the rest of the company about the marketplace.)
- Market trends do not always emerge because data is often not aggregated across all sales situations.

The Organizational Challenges of Prospect Feedback Information Sharing

- Organizational challenges also cause distortions in information sharing because many companies play the adult version of the telephone whisper game.
- Hierarchical and political factors further inhibit information sharing, as not all employees feel comfortable discussing and debating critical issues with senior management.

Why Companies Suffer from Strategic Misalignment

- Not understanding what prospects are looking for and not having this information readily available can create strategic misalignment in your company's products, services, pricing, sales process, marketing/branding, and strategy.

How to Implement a Win/Loss Program

In Appendix B we will explore how to implement a successful win/loss program guaranteed to increase your sales team's new business win rate. This appendix offers a practical, highly targeted, and easy-to-implement solution that can pay huge dividends over time for any company.

This appendix has two sections. In the first section, we will review five key factors you should consider before implementing a program for your sales team. In section two, we will show you a step by step process for implementing a win/loss program.

First, let's explore how to get started by examining some key factors to consider before you implement a program.

FIVE FACTORS TO CONSIDER BEFORE IMPLEMENTING A PROGRAM

The first step of the process is to decide on the program parameters and then work on getting buy-in from all relevant areas of your company. This will ensure that the program is strategically integrated within your organization.

Here are five things to consider before you implement a program:

1. What parameters will your program cover (e.g., product segments, target markets, territories, deal sizes)?

2. What is the best type of interview protocol (phone, Internet, paper, face to face)?
3. Will your organization manage this work internally or externally?
4. Does the program have the necessary executive-level sponsorship and comprehensive buy-in from all critical areas of your company?
5. Will the program be well integrated with existing processes of your company on an ongoing basis?

Let's explore each of these foundational factors in more detail.

What Parameters Will Your Program Cover?

Let's review four program parameters you should establish before you implement a program:

1. *Product/service segments.* One important decision you must make is which of your company's products or services you will include in the win/loss program. For example, win/loss research can be extremely valuable when a company is rolling out a new product or service. Getting feedback at an early stage of product launch can be very valuable and can save your company considerable time and money. Often the learning that can be gained by early win/loss research can substantially increase your knowledge level and success (a feat that might take years to achieve).

   Often companies will start a win/loss program in one specific area and expand the program into other areas over time. This can occur once the methodology has been proven and actionable success has been achieved. Some companies will focus on their core products; others will focus on new product initiatives. All of these factors should be considerations when starting a win/loss program.

2. *Target markets.* Win/loss research can also be valuable when a company is entering a new market segment or target market. For example, your company may have a significant

business working with a certain type of customer but not much experience with another type of client. Therefore, you can conduct win/loss research as you begin to bid for these different customers in new target markets. These interviews are often eye-opening and highlight a totally different paradigm and sales process that sales teams are all too often unprepared for. However, the end result quickly clarifies the nuances of the new competitive landscape and helps you to reach your sales goals much faster than you would have if you "learned the hard way" over a protracted period of time.

3. *Territories/geographies.* You can also choose to focus on specific territories or geographic areas. For instance, sales may be declining in a particular part of the country and senior executives may not know why. Therefore, with a more targeted and segmented analysis, the true issues can emerge and clarity can be gained. This allows for faster implementation of solutions.

4. *Deal size.* In addition to product segments, target markets, and territories, another key thing to think about when designing a win/loss program is which sales situations will be included based on the size of the prospect. Many companies choose to focus on their largest sales situations above a minimum revenue threshold.

For example, your company may be involved with various sized customers. Some prospects may be large and represent significant revenue opportunities while other prospects may be small. Therefore, you may want to consider performing interviews only above a certain revenue threshold. For example, you may want to interview only prospects that represent more than $25,000 in annual revenue to your company.

This is not to say that smaller prospects are not important. In fact, many companies will interview a portion of smaller deal situations as a complement to larger deal research. This can help you compare and contrast the sales process as well as your company's products and services by market segment. Many times clients can gain significant perspective by segmenting the results in this fashion, and synergies can be gained by learning lessons from each type of deal size situation.

Once you have decided on your program parameters, you will next need to determine what type of interview protocol makes the most sense for your sales process.

What Is the Best Type of Interview Protocol?

Most win/loss research is conducted via the telephone, but depending on what industry you are in and how long and costly your sales cycle is, this can vary. In general, your chosen interview methodology will depend on four key factors:

1. The length of your sales cycle
2. The revenue potential/dollar value of each deal won and lost
3. The dollar value of how much it takes to sell a deal (selling expenses)
4. Your budget for the win/loss analysis program

For a product with a short sales cycle, low sales costs, and low revenue, a paper or Web survey may suffice. For example, when you sell a car, your sales cycle may take one afternoon, and the sales cost and revenue may be low in comparison to other products or services. In this case, paper or Web surveys are probably adequate. That said, paper and Web surveys are a tricky way to get prospect feedback on any given sales process because this methodology does not allow for any probing or detailed dialogues with prospects. Paper and Web surveys work much better for client/customer satisfaction surveys.

However, if you are in an industry with, say, a three- to nine-month sales cycle, it costs your company $10,000 to $25,000 in expenses to sell a deal, and the final contract can earn your company $25,000 to $250,000 in annual revenue, a phone interview is probably the best course of action.

Last, if you are in an industry where your sales cycle is very long (say, one to two years), it costs your company a significant amount of money to go after business (say, more than $100,000 per deal), and each deal is worth more than $500,000 in revenue, an in-person interview may be warranted. Much of this will depend on the proximity of the prospect in relation to your company.

The type of interviews your company chooses to conduct will also depend on your budget as well as the specifics of your industry. In all, phone interviews have proven to be the most used and versatile form of getting feedback from prospects. Speaking with a prospect over the phone is usually the most cost effective way to gather data while also allowing for probing on specifics issues. Face-to-face interviews are also much more costly to conduct because of the logistics of getting the interviewer to the prospect's office, a cumbersome situation for a company with a national business.

Will Your Organization Manage This Program Internally or Externally?

The next decision you will need to make before implementing a win/loss program for your business is whether you will perform this work internally (by using research or marketing areas separate from sales) or use an outside third party to perform the research. As Appendix A showed, there are many reasons you should consider hiring an outside provider to perform this strategic initiative. These include

1. *Ability to obtain independent, unbiased, and candid information.* As we explored in Part 1, there are many reasons that salespeople don't receive candid feedback from prospects. By using an independent third party, you essentially eliminate these challenges. First, because an independent interviewer is conducting the debriefs, you have eliminated all salesperson issues or biases since they are simply not involved. Second, prospects can now feel free to vent and give candid feedback because they have no relationship to the third party and therefore can feel more at ease with giving constructive feedback.

   Additionally, as we have addressed, on average, 38 percent of new business lost is the direct result of issues with the salesperson or sales process. Therefore, by giving prospects a comfortable environment in which to provide feedback, you will allow them to express their sales process issues candidly, in a constructive way. Last, prospects feel more at ease divulging competitive information to a third-party interviewer. All of these things allow for a much more comprehensive postdecision sales debrief to occur. Whether you ask your salespeople to perform this research or use your own internal company resources, you simply will not be able to gather as much candid information as a qualified third-party researcher.

True, if your sales team implements the techniques from this book, they will do a better job at gathering data, but as a sales manager, you still have the challenge of aggregating this data with process consistency across your sales team—no small task.

2. *Ability for prospects to remain anonymous.* By hiring an outside firm to conduct interviews and analyze and present the results, you are also offering your prospects one very valuable option for providing feedback—the option to remain anonymous during their discussions. By allowing prospects to truly remain anonymous during their discussions, you are providing them with additional latitude to be as candid and as forthcoming as possible. This allows for even more actionable information to be acquired.

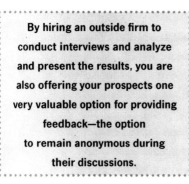

By hiring an outside firm to conduct interviews and analyze and present the results, you are also offering your prospects one very valuable option for providing feedback—the option to remain anonymous during their discussions.

3. *Experience.* Outside consulting and market research firms that conduct this work can have significant experience in win/loss research and can therefore design surveys, conduct interviews, and perform analysis at a higher level than can typically be performed internally. By using an expert outside third party, you will be able to tap in to a firm that understands how to collect and analyze data. Outside firms will also have perfected their methodologies and will understand how to best contact prospects, while in-house employees may be performing this work for the first time

and therefore will not gain any synergies from past work. When work is performed in-house, people often only view the work as conducting a series of interviews instead of as being part of a larger strategic process.

4. *Resources.* Outside firms will also have the resources and a trained and dedicated staff to conduct the research and manage the program. Frequently, when companies try to conduct win/loss work internally, it can get pushed aside for more immediate pressing "fire drills." When win/loss gets performed only when time permits, much of the strategic benefit of the program is lost. The value comes from consistently monitoring prospect feedback. Additionally, many in-house programs find out that they are more costly and time consuming than originally anticipated; therefore, outside firms can actually be a more cost-effective solution while providing more actionable and relevant information.

5. *Reporting.* An outside firm's ability to provide in-depth reporting is also a significant benefit versus more limited reporting available in house. Often when results are presented by in-house market researchers, they are presented in raw form with only top line results. Outside firms also generally have an industry specific specialty that allows them to present the results with more success.

Table B.1 encapsulates the major differences between hiring a third party and conducting win/loss research in house.

Although using an outside third party is the preferred methodology, budgetary circumstances may dictate that you need to assign someone within your organization to manage and run this program. The best type of person to manage and perform win/loss work internally is someone from the product or marketing area. Product or marketing interviewers are the most logical choice because after sales, they may have the most to gain from acquiring this information. Additionally, they

> The best type of person to manage and perform win/loss work internally is someone from the product or marketing area.

Benefits of hiring outside third party:	Common pitfalls when using internal resources:
➤ Independent, unbiased perspective.	➤ Often hidden biases.
➤ Gives prospects/new clients option of remaining truly anonymous to the company.	➤ Prospects/clients are never truly anonymous to the company. Even if anonymity is requested, prospects tend to feel less secure about their comments remaining confidential from the sales team.
➤ Experience conducting these types of studies/data analysis.	➤ Generally there is a lack of experience among internal staff with this particular type of work.
➤ Experienced staff who are trained in speaking with similar clients/prospects.	➤ Lack of experience with this type of interview limits ability to effectively probe/alter line of questioning based on prospect's unique answers.
➤ Focus on conducting this type of work.	➤ Often juggling multiple priorities; win/loss is not main focus.
➤ Aggregate data, analyze results from a statistical perspective and put together comprehensive report of the findings.	➤ Limited analysis performed. Often results are reported in raw, statistical numbers vs. in-depth analysis and segmentation of results.

Table B.1

will already have significant knowledge regarding your company's products or services. Lastly, marketing areas often fall under the purview of the sales organization; therefore, they may have a working knowledge of how the sales process works. Be sure that whoever conducts the interviews has a strong phone voice and is not afraid to get people on the phone and make discussions happen.

Once you have decided whether you will manage this work internally or externally, your next step is to ensure that you have the necessary executive-level sponsorship and buy-in from all critical areas of your company.

Does the Program Have Executive-Level Sponsorship?

Once you have decided who will run the program, what parameters the program will cover, and what type of interviews you will conduct, you next need to ensure that you educate all the relevant areas of your company and gain consensus and buy-in for the program.

In order for a win/loss program to work, it must have executive-level sponsorship. If the president of your company or general manager of your business area is not committed to the program and does not understand the long-term value and effect of a successful program, then it will be hard for you to make the program a success.

The reason for this is that win/loss analysis will involve and impact almost every area of your company. Win/loss "crossfertilizes" across sales, marketing, product development, technology, client service, operations, pricing, and so on. Therefore, anyone who has direct oversight over all or each of these areas must be behind the process. If there is no buy-in from the top of your company to conduct a win/loss study, it can become challenging politically for the organization to work together. The feedback gained is worthless if not acted upon. This is perhaps the biggest reason win/loss programs fail.

> In order for a win/loss program to work, it must have executive-level sponsorship.

This is why it is crucial to make sure that whoever is running your business is involved in the decision-making process up front and has given her sponsorship to the program. Without this, all the other areas may not work together to make the program a success.

The second key organizational success factor of a win/loss program is to get buy-in for the program across the organization, especially within the senior management team. It is critical that all areas of your company are on board with the process and are committed to the program's success. Everyone who is directly or indirectly impacted by this research must know that this type of feedback is vital to the long-term learning and strategic success of the company. If people don't feel a sense of ownership at the senior levels of the company, they often don't participate in making the program a success.

One interesting barrier can occur when one area begins the program and doesn't get buy-in from other areas. For example, one classic problem occurs when the marketing or product area initiates and performs win/loss research. This often creates problems and defensiveness from the sales side of the organization. The reason for this is that sales (and the head of sales in particular) may feel threatened to have another area getting feedback on their sales team and sales process. In these cases, it is particularly critical to ensure that the sales organization is "on board" with the program.

When win/loss is conducted by an area other than sales, it often causes conflict in many ways. The biggest way this stifles the program is because the sales team may not be willing to offer up the prospect data necessary to make the program a success (if this data is not accessible on some form of CRM database). Also, sales may not be accepting of the results because they were not involved in the design of the survey and programs. By contrast, the marketing and product development areas may feel intimidated and brushed aside by sales because of this situation.

One final thing to consider is whether your organization will mainly use this information as a learning and knowledge tool, or as an individual performance metric. You do not want this research to come across as a "witch hunt," whereby salespeople will be evaluated on their performance during the interviews. Instead, focus it more as a learning exercise that will facilitate knowledge sharing throughout the organization. Some companies do choose to use win/loss as a way to rate and monitor their sales forces but this is up to each individual company to decide and largely depends on the culture of the organization.

You must have support from all levels of your organization; otherwise the program will not survive over the long run.

Will the Program Be Integrated with Your Company's Existing Processes?

Another important factor for success is positioning the program as a long-term process, not a one-time occurrence. Some companies feel that they can conduct a study once and then do not have to do it again. This is false thinking, because in order for a win/loss program to be effective, it must be part of a long-term process. It can take a while before an organization begins to click into the program and really start to make meaningful changes to its products, services, and sales process.

Think of win/loss as an exercise program for your company. Just as you can't expect to go to the gym for a month and be in shape for the rest of your life, you can't expect to perform win/loss once and get your company in shape. Getting into great physical shape is a process that entails a continuous lifestyle of regular exercise, healthy nutrition, good sleep, etc. Win/loss should be looked at the same way. If you want your company

> Just as you can't expect to go to the gym for a month and be in shape for the rest of your life, you can't expect to perform win/loss once and get your company in shape.

to be in good shape, you have to keep it on an exercise regimen. In order for your company to stay healthy, it must be exercising all the time.

To maximize effectiveness, win/loss must be integrated into the regular workings of your organization. For example, in terms of prospect data collection, win/loss works best if it is integrated with your current CRM database (if you have one). If you are using SalesForce.com, it would be best if your win/loss program can gather the prospect data from SalesForce.com.

Additionally, win/loss interviews should be shared with individual sales team members, not just sales and senior management. Often regional sales managers or the heads of sales do not share the information with the sales teams. This is a huge lost opportunity to teach your individual salespeople the reasons they are winning and losing.

Another example of integration is having an annual presentation of the results to all areas involved in the senior management team. Additionally, quarterly or semiannual reporting also helps to keep win/loss results front and center in everyone's minds as they make their daily decisions.

Last, win/loss analysis should be tied in to your company's annual strategic planning process. If you are not factoring in feedback from prospects and marketplace perceptions into your annual strategic planning, you are missing a huge opportunity to align your strategy more accurately to the marketplace.

There are many things to think about before getting started. However, if you successfully address each of these questions, you will have built a great foundation for developing a successful program. Now that we have explored these areas, let's review how to implement a win/loss program.

HOW TO IMPLEMENT A WIN/LOSS ANALYSIS PROGRAM

Once you've identified the target population for the interviews, the interview methodology, who will be responsible for conducting the win/loss work (i.e., internal versus external), and once you have established support from all levels of the organization, you are ready to start implementing a program.

(Please note that this section provides details with the assumption that an outside third-party research firm will be used. If this is not how you choose to operate your program, you can simply disregard the sections that reference using an outside party.)

The implementation of a win/loss analysis program involves the following seven steps:

1. Identify an internal program coordinator to work with your chosen "external" win/loss research firm.
2. Set up a kickoff meeting to get all relevant parties together to go over project parameters, survey design, and workflow.
3. Train your win/loss firm (and their interviewers) on your company's sales process, products, and client service delivery model.
4. Design and finalize your interview questionnaire with relevant personnel.
5. Determine how to provide ongoing deal information on recent wins and losses.
6. Conduct and write up interviews and disseminate to relevant personnel.
7. Aggregate findings and present to company management/relevant personnel.

Let's explore each of these steps in more detail.

1. Identify an Internal Program Coordinator

The first thing you'll need to do when implementing a win/loss program is to identify an internal program coordinator (often someone in the sales or marketing organization) to work with the "external" win/loss firm. This internal program coordinator will be the go-to person and will be responsible for working directly with the outside win/loss research firm and the sales team to get deal information and finalize research instruments.

It is absolutely critical to assign the right type of person to this role. This internal program coordinator must be someone who can get things done and has enough authority to ensure that different areas of the company work together. This person must also feel comfortable speaking to and working with salespeople because he or she will need to be able to collect and extract deal flow information from the sales team. This can be a challenging situation for anyone since some salespeople may not want to be totally forthcoming with respect to handing over their won or lost deal situations.

Some companies choose to assign personnel with more administrative backgrounds to coordinate this type of program. This usually does not work very well because the sales team sometimes ignores the attempts of less senior personnel within the company. Instead, try to find someone the salespeople already have a relationship with and respect. This will ensure successful data collection from the sales team. For example, if your company fills out RFPs as part of the sales process for prospects, whoever oversees this area often has much of the prospect data necessary to conduct win/loss interviews, and he or she typically is very involved with and has relationships with all members of the sales team.

Please note: if your company is able to gather deal flow information from a CRM database, then it is less necessary that the program coordinator be as involved with the sales team.

2. Set up a Kickoff Meeting with All Relevant Parties

Now that you have selected the right internal program coordinator, you should work with your outside win/loss research firm to set up a program kickoff meeting. Anyone who will be involved or impacted by this program should attend this meeting. Also, it is critical the head of sales be at this meeting so this person understands everything the program entails.

This meeting should be used to introduce your outside win/loss firm to your program coordinator as well as to all personnel within the company involved in the program. This meeting should cover all of the program parameters reviewed in the first section of this appendix as well as specific questions your team would like addressed during the research. Survey design and workflow should also be clearly explained to all attendees. In short, after this meeting, everyone involved should fully understand why win/loss is necessary and how the program will work. Your outside win/loss firm should be able to lead this meeting.

3. Train Your Win/Loss Firm and Its Interviewers

The next step in the process is to train the external third party responsible for running the program. If you hire an outside third party, you should provide them with training and information pertinent to your company. This could include such things as sales and marketing materials that describe your product and service offerings, organizational charts, past interview transcripts (if you've performed any win/loss work in the past), a sample RFP response, and internal training documents that describe relevant processes and procedures pertaining to your sales strategy and approach.

The interviews will run smoother, and the person conducting the interviews will sound more professional, if you provide ample time on the front end to familiarize your chosen win/loss researchers with your company and its sales process.

4. Design and Finalize Interview Questionnaire

We discussed earlier in this appendix the importance of having buy-in from all levels of the organization as well as all internal departments and areas that will be affected by the research. The best way to achieve this is to allow these key parties to be included in the design of the interview questionnaire.

The best way to approach this is to have your win/loss firm draft an initial questionnaire and submit it to the relevant personnel in the sales organization who will be responsible for reviewing it. Once the sales organization is comfortable with the document, they should then forward it to the other areas of the company that will benefit from the research. For example, marketing, operations, and client service will all likely be involved in some aspect of the sales process, so having their buy-in on the survey design will be of benefit. These areas often have valuable perspectives and may have additional questions they'd like to ask. This process will reduce if not eliminate defensiveness pertaining to the results of the program since these other areas of the company will feel they too are owners of the research.

It may take several drafts before the questionnaire is fully customized to your company's unique needs, so make sure you are patient and get input from all areas of the company. Additionally, it is easy to change the survey as the program evolves, so don't feel as though you can't make ongoing alterations to the survey.

5. Determine How to Gather Ongoing Deal Information

The next step is for your internal program coordinator to identify how to best acquire and forward the necessary sales information to the person conducting the interviews. The best way to do this so that you avoid biases in terms of the deals you submit is to take the information straight from a CRM database (if your company uses one). For example, if your company uses SalesForce.com, you should gather the prospect data straight from the database. This will not only ensure that the deal information is submitted in a timely fashion, but it will also eliminate the potential conflict of interest of salespeople cherry-picking deals to send in.

If you do not have a CRM database or spreadsheet where pertinent deal information is collected, you may need to rely on your sales force to submit this information. If this is the case, be sure there is someone in a managerial role overseeing this process and making sure that deals are not being deliberately excluded. It is often difficult for a manager to know every deal that her sales teams are involved in, but it is imperative that each salesperson be held accountable for submitting an unbiased sampling of recent wins and losses.

Often wins are easier to collect since your company will know which prospects have become customers, but the losses will present a greater challenge. If you are using an outside third party, ask them to provide a status report by salesperson each month so that the internal coordinator/sales managers can review it and identify which salespeople are not providing adequate deal flow.

6. Conduct and Disseminate Interviews

Once everyone has come to agreement on the interview questionnaire, the interviewers from the win/loss firm should conduct a handful of interviews and coordinate a conference call with the internal program coordinator to review the first few to make sure they are garnering adequate and relevant information. If there are things that are not coming through clearly in the interviews, or if there are questions that need to be changed, it is best to catch such problems at the beginning of the program so that everyone is on the same page moving forward.

Additionally, it is important to determine which internal parties should be included on the interview dissemination list. The interviews (particularly the losses) will undoubtedly contain sensitive information, so the initial distribution list should be rather select. From there, sales managers should decide how to get the feedback to each individual salesperson.

One of the most important elements in this process is to get the feedback to the sales team. The primary purpose of this program is to help each salesperson improve his performance and increase his new business win rate. It is extremely difficult for salespeople to do this effectively if they are not getting unfiltered feedback on a consistent basis. At a

> Having your salespeople read their own win/loss transcripts is analogous to having a football team review game tapes.

minimum, each salesperson who was involved in a deal should be able to read their interviews in real time.

Just as sports teams review game tapes, sales teams and companies must do the same to prepare for upcoming presentations. Sports teams review game tapes because it is hard to analyze defeat (or victory) while the players are in the middle of the game. Time, perspective, and distance allow sports teams to gather and reflect on what happened and what needs to be improved upon in the next game of the season. It's the same for sales teams, as it is often impossible to dissect areas for improvement fully while you are within a given sales process. Having your salespeople read their own win/loss transcripts is analogous to having a football team review game tapes.

Ultimately, win/loss works best when a company receives the interviews on a real-time basis. This allows for a continuous and real-time stream of prospect and marketplace feedback.

One final note: when prospects are followed up with for feedback, make sure it is done in a timely fashion. The best time to speak with a prospect is roughly two to four weeks after his buying decision has been made. This will ensure that you get the best data because the details of the buying process will still be fresh in the prospect's mind. It is critical to

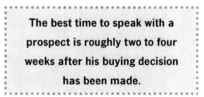

The best time to speak with a prospect is roughly two to four weeks after his buying decision has been made.

follow up with prospects no later than two months after the buying decision has been made. If you speak with a prospect after two months has gone by, you will generally find that he has forgotten critical differentiation points of the sales process.

7. Aggregate Findings and Present to Senior Management

The final step of the program involves aggregating all the interview data and presenting the findings to senior management and other relevant personnel. This type of data analysis should, at a minimum, be pulled together annually. That said, a semiannual analysis will better enable the company to identify trends in the data over time.

As mentioned, the interviews should be disseminated and studied as soon as they are completed to allow the sales team to benefit on a real-time basis. It is also important, however, to aggregate the data and quantify the results to provide management with a full analysis of what is going right and what needs improvement across the entire sales team and company.

If the program is to be impactful at all levels of the organization, it is imperative that the findings be rolled up in aggregate and thoroughly analyzed. While the verbatim feedback that each interview transcript provides is instrumental in helping sales teams learn from their individual experiences, the sales organization as a whole will benefit far more if it is able to learn from all of the company's sales experiences in aggregate.

Tracking performance year over year is another important component of win/loss analysis. This allows companies to look at whether or not their work on "fixing" issues and realigning strategies is paying off. Year-to-year analysis can be tracked on an absolute basis as well as relative to the competition. In highly competitive industries, improvements are generally made year over year, and the competitive landscape will evolve and change as well. Proactively monitoring this activity will ensure that your company is keeping pace with the industry and reacting to changes in real time.

APPENDIX WRAP-UP

In his book *Good to Great*, Jim Collins (New York: HarperCollins, 2001) discusses many principles that relate perfectly to the concept of a win/loss analysis program. His book highlights the fact that great companies always engage in spirited debate and healthy conflict. They focus on performing "autopsies" without blame and confront the brutal facts about themselves and their marketplace. Additionally, they set up what he calls "red flag mechanisms" that serve to warn the company in advance when problems are on the horizon.

He also establishes that great companies commit to continuous improvement and focus on the process of improvement instead of looking for the one big "aha" moment or plan. Great companies have discipline and work day by day toward results, and they don't shy away from the brutal facts. Instead, they seek to understand them fully and work toward addressing the issues.

A win/loss analysis program is a perfect management tool for companies because it provides information that can be used in the ways that Jim Collins sets forth in his book. Win/loss analysis provides the brutal facts through an actionable red flag mechanism. A win/loss program also helps companies engage in debate in a more healthy and productive way because when an independent third party is used to perform the research, all employees will be working from the same candid information. Everyone will be working off the same data, percentages, and positive and negative feedback. Therefore, organizations will not need to spend time pontificating about problem areas and won't need to wade through the noise and the clutter of everyone's opinions. Instead, a company's senior management team can focus on solving problems. The amount of time this saves companies is immense, but it works only if a company has discipline and commits to continuous improvement over time.

APPENDIX SUMMARY

Five Factors to Consider before Implementing a Win/Loss Analysis Program

- What are the parameters your program will cover (i.e., product segments, target markets, territories, and deal sizes)?
- What is the best type of interview protocol (i.e., phone, Internet, paper, face to face)?
- Will your organization perform this work internally or externally?
- Does the program have the necessary executive level sponsorship and comprehensive buy-in from all critical areas of your company?
- Will the program be well integrated with existing processes of your company on an ongoing basis?

How to Implement a Win/Loss Analysis Program

The implementation of a win/loss analysis program involves the following seven steps:

1. Identify an internal program coordinator to work with your chosen "external" win/loss research firm.
2. Set up a kickoff meeting to get all relevant parties together to go over project parameters, survey design, and workflow.
3. Train your win/loss firm (and its interviewers) on your company's sales process, product offerings, and client service delivery model.
4. Design and finalize the interview questionnaire with relevant personnel.
5. Determine how to provide ongoing deal information on recent wins and losses.
6. Conduct and write up interviews and disseminate to relevant personnel.
7. Aggregate findings and present to company management/relevant personnel.

Index

CPSIA information can be obtained at www.ICGtesting.com
Printed in the USA
BVOW04s0926090514

353025BV00006B/16/P

9 780071 718110